CONTENTS

RECRUITING LIBRARY STAFF

A How-To-Do-It Manual for Librarians

Kathleen Low

HOW-TO-DO-IT MANUALS FOR LIBRARIANS

NUMBER 94

NEAL-SCHUMAN PUBLISHERS, INC.
New York, London

Published by Neal-Schuman Publishers, Inc.
100 Varick Street
New York, NY 10013

Printed and bound in the United States of America.

Library of Congress Cataloging-in-Publication Data

Low, Kathleen.
    Recruiting library staff : a how-to-do-it manual for librarians / Kathleen Low.
       p.   cm. — (How-to-do-it manuals for librarians; no. 94)
    Includes bibliographical references (p.).
    ISBN 1-55570-355-0
    1. Library employees—Recruiting—United States. I. Title.
II. Series : How-to-do-it manuals for libraries ; no. 94.
Z282.35.R42L69   1999
023'.9—dc21   99–31281
                                                    CIP

FIGURES

WORKSHEETS

PREFACE

In libraries and organizations everywhere, there is likely to be someone who sucks the enthusiasm and dedication out of the best staff members. These problem staff are worse than annoying. Whereas quality staff can raise the image, credibility, efficiency, and effectiveness of your library, problem staff can quickly destroy your library's credibility and the value of your library to the community, college, corporation, or organization it strives to serve.

The best way to avoid problem staff members is never to hire them into your library. This may sound easy, but as you know, it is not. The degree of difficulty in recruiting the brightest and best depends on the extent of your skill in recruitment. Yes, recruitment is a skill—one of the most important skills you can possess to ensure the library's continued vitality. Fortunately, like all skills, effective recruitment can be learned.

Recruiting Library Staff: A How-To-Do-It Manual for Librarians presents the practical "how-to" information needed to develop the knowledge and skills for effective staff recruitment. *Recruiting Library Staff* is intended for all levels of library staff who may be called upon to participate in the recruitment process. It is also aimed at personnel or human resources staff who may be unfamiliar with recruiting applicants for library positions.

Because every staff member a library patron comes into contact with is a representative of the library, *Recruiting Library Staff* does not distinguish between professional and nonprofessional staff. The techniques discussed apply to the recruitment of custodial staff as well as high-level management positions. Every single staff member, regardless of classification, contributes to the overall success of the library in fulfilling its mission.

Reading *Recruiting Library Staff* will help the library staff member gain an understanding of how recruitment works—how to write an informative description of the desired staff member, decide whether to use search firms or attend job fairs, advertise successfully, network, and implement a successful recruitment process. In addition, the would-be recruiter learns how to present the library as a desirable employer, select a positive library image and project it, and use future job vacancies as starting points for effective recruitment.

Chapter 1, "Introduction: The Recruitment Process," provides an overview of the recruitment process.

Chapter 2, "Portraying Your Library as a Good Employer," takes the reader through an exercise in identifying potential reasons why applicants may find the library an attractive place to seek employment. The reasons, many of them ignored by most libraries, range from benefits to the library's proximity to recreation activities or shopping.

Chapter 3, "Determining Current and Future Openings," is a guide to the process of conducting a job analysis and developing or revising job descriptions for vacant positions. Chapter 3 stresses the importance of a job audit, the review and revision of the job description whenever a position is vacated, and the relevance of job audits and job descriptions to effective recruitment.

Chapter 4, "Determining the General Skills and Characteristics of Individuals You Seek to Recruit," addresses methods for identifying skills and characteristics with some simple questions, provides lists of skills and characteristics commonly sought after, and gives advice on the necessary knowledge of relevant legal issues.

Chapter 5, "Selecting the Library Image You Wish to Promote" is a practical approach to understanding the importance of image and how to promote a positive image, along with Six Steps in Determining and Selecting the Image You Want to Promote and Seven Tips to Enhancing Your Library's Image.

Chapter 6, "Using the Best Recruitment Methods," looks at the range of available recruitment methods. These options range from advertising and on-campus recruiting to executive search firms. The advantages and disadvantages of each method, as well as potential costs, are highlighted.

Chapter 7, "Recruitment Advertising," discusses the advertising process. Four Crucial Questions regarding goals, number of vacancies, advertising resources, and time constraints are followed by Five Steps to Developing a Recruitment Advertisement. Because advertising costs can consume significant budget dollars, advertising cost worksheets are included to aid in calculating expected costs.

Chapter 8, "Maximizing Your Participation in Job Events," will help you make the most of your staff and financial investments in job events. This chapter is helpful in determining display needs, discovering how to make the most of job fairs, purchasing premiums and giveaways, and avoiding serious mistakes.

Chapter 9, "Networking for Recruitment Purposes," highlights the benefits of networking and explains how to network effectively with Five Basic Steps.

The book can be read through cover to cover, or opened to any aspect of recruitment that requires attention. In either case, you will gain maximum benefit from *Recruiting Library Staff* by asking yourself the suggested questions, working through the step-by-step guides in light of your institution's mission, and remaining open to change in your recruitment procedures and to the staff who are involved. In this way, you increase your chances of attracting a high caliber applicant pool, so that when you get to the interview stage you will have the opportunity of choosing from several attractive candidates.

1 INTRODUCTION: THE RECRUITMENT PROCESS

Good staff can raise an organization, business, or library to new heights of success. Bad staff can sink an organization beyond salvation. Libraries frequently fail to recognize the importance of the staff recruitment process and fail to allocate sufficient resources to this activity. For those libraries faced with declining budgets, staff recruitment generally takes a back seat to finding new methods of increasing the library's budget. However, recruitment of the "right" staff is often vital to increasing the library's budget. The addition of staff with crucial political, financial, public awareness, or outreach skills may be just what the library needs to help realize increased funding. Since staff are an organization's greatest asset, staff recruitment deserves the attention of all staff, from the library director on down. Recruitment is a highly competitive activity and should not be relegated solely to personnel departments or individuals.

There are several key individuals within the library whose participation is paramount to the library's success in recruiting the best and the brightest staff. Although the library's personnel or human resources office handles the actual recruitment tasks—such as posting job openings, receiving and screening applications, scheduling interviews, and ensuring compliance with current law—the staff in this office are just a few of the many individuals who need to play a key role in the process.

Yes, recruitment is a process. The process outlined in this chapter will enable you to define and develop your recruitment activities (a summary is highlighted in the box). Anyone can follow the process. However, the more skilled you are at the process, the more effective you'll be at attracting the top-notch applicants. Developing your skill in this area simply requires dedication, persistence, patience, and the willingness to take the time to learn what works, what doesn't, and to modify your activities and thinking accordingly. As we move through the various steps in this process, we will also take a close look at the people within the library who need to be involved in each of these steps and why (see Figure 1–1).

SEVEN STEPS TO SUCCESSFUL RECRUITING

STEP 1. SEEK ADMINISTRATIVE SUPPORT AND VISION

The first step in the recruitment process is to establish ongoing communication and a good rapport with the library or the larger organization's administrators and executive officers. You need their support for your recruitment activities. This support should include the allocation of adequate budget and personnel resources to the recruitment function. You also need them to communicate the importance of the recruitment function to all library staff, and to support and assist in the efforts as needed.

Equally important, you need the organization's executives and administrators to provide you with their vision. Learn where they intend to lead the organization into the future. Have them articulate the type of staff they believe the library needs to make that vision a reality.

This Step Needs the Involvement of: The Director of the Library

No recruitment efforts will be successful without the involvement of the library director. Bringing in the executive with ultimate oversight over the library and its budget is critical to the success of both the recruitment and retention of library staff. He, or she, provides the strategic direction and vision for the library and defines the role of the library in supporting or furthering the vision of its parent organization (such as the corporation, city, or the like). The director is essential in providing the library resources needed to recruit individuals who can help fulfill the library and the organization's visions. The director also communicates the importance of the recruitment function to management and insures participation and support by library managers for various recruitment activities involving library staff at all levels.

Seven Steps to Successful Recruiting

1. Seek administrative support and vision.
2. Determine your staffing needs.
3. Determine your target audience.
4. Select the best recruitment method.
5. Identify the positive aspects of your library as an employer.
6. Recruit.
7. Evaluate, refine, and continue recruiting.

Figure 1–1 Checklist: Who Should be Involved, and in What Role?	
Who	**Involvement / Role**
Director	• Provides vision and strategic direction for the library • Communicates importance of recruitment efforts to managers and staff • Insures workplace quality and an environment conducive to employee development and retention
Personnel office	• Hire staff who can help the library attain its vision, within existing employment laws
Managers	• Assist personnel office in applicant recruitment and employee selection • Insure that supervisors complete a job audit / assessment of positions to be vacated • Oversee and insure ongoing library staff development efforts • Create and maintain a desirable work environment
Supervisors	• Complete job audits / assessments of positions to be vacated to insure effective recruitment of individuals with the skills and knowledge necessary to successfully perform the job
All library staff	• Assist in identification of potential internal and external applicants • Serve as library representatives to potential applicants

In addition, the director sets the tone within the workplace and is crucial to employee retention. Retention is an integral part of the recruitment effort, since organizations with a reputation for having a "revolving door" for employees have difficulty recruiting quality staff. It's vital to get the "buy-in" of the director in the overall recruitment process, which is affected by employee development, training, opportunities for advancement, as well as library working conditions. The director needs to be alerted to and involved in employee development and retention issues, which can impact the employee turnover rate. Given the cost of employee recruitment, issues regarding retention need to be addressed by the director.

STEP 2. DETERMINE YOUR STAFFING NEEDS

The next step in the recruitment process is determining what your library's staffing needs are. You can't even begin to recruit the ideal employees until you know what you're looking for. Identify all current job vacancies to be filled and those positions expected to become vacant in the near future. This needs to occur on an ongoing basis.

For each vacancy or expected vacancy, conduct a job analysis to determine the responsibilities and need for the specific position. Then, in collaboration with the supervisor of the position, and if possible the incumbent, determine and prioritize the specific skills, experience, and characteristics an individual needs to possess to be successful in the position.

This Step Needs the Involvement of: The Library Managers, the Personnel Office

Library Managers

Library managers, although key players in the recruitment process, frequently fail to view themselves as vital players in the recruitment process. However, their role is far greater than that of the supervisor of the employee to be hired. The managers' responsibilities include the effective management of all personnel within their unit or department. This includes ensuring supervisors complete a job audit (an assessment of positions expected to be vacated in the near future) and work with unit supervisors to identify and modify any aspects of vacant positions to better meet the needs of the unit and the library.

The library manager can and actively should assist the personnel office in selecting appropriate avenues for promoting availability of vacant positions. Whereas the personnel office is knowledgeable of various mechanisms for advertising openings, such as in newspapers and magazines, the library manager, as a library professional, is often aware of specific professional avenues (such as newsletters of specialized library groups, Internet listservs, joblines) that may yield a smaller number of applicants but ones more qualified for the position.

Because library managers are accountable for the work environment in their departments, their involvement in the recruitment process and in creating an attractive workplace is critical to successful, long-term recruitment efforts. The most desirable applicants have the luxury of being able to select among the potential employers. Only those libraries able to offer an enticing work environment will be able to compete for these employees.

Personnel Office

The specific role played by the personnel office varies depending upon its overall function within the institution or organization. In some organizations, a personnel office exists solely for the purpose of hiring of new employees, managing employee benefits, and handling personnel transactions. In some organizations, the personnel office also encompasses an entire spectrum of human resource development functions, which include activities such as employee orientation and staff training, conducting job audits, or training managers in how to conduct them. In either case, the most important role of the personnel office is to insure the proper hiring of staff who can assist the library in attaining its vision. This responsibility includes oversight of the entire recruitment and hiring process, and insuring it complies with existing employment laws.

STEP 3. DETERMINE YOUR TARGET AUDIENCE

Now that you've identified your job vacancies, and the skills, characteristics, and experiences sought in applicants to fill those positions, it's time to zoom in on your recruitment target audiences. Are you seeking applicants with bilingual skills, advanced technical skills, entry-level clerical skills, or do you need entry-level children's librarians? Is your target audience from a specific geographic area? Is your target audience a certain age group?

This Step Needs the Involvement of: The Personnel Office

Your personnel office can assist you in this step, and may have past experience in defining the target audiences.

STEP 4. SELECT THE BEST RECRUITMENT METHOD

After identifying your target audience, it's time to decide on the best method or methods for reaching that audience. These methods range from advertising in a variety of media to on-campus recruiting to using executive search firms. Your decision on what method(s) to select will in part depend upon your recruitment budget, staff resources, and initial comfort level with the various methods. Just remember not to limit yourself to the methods you start with. Although you may at first decide to follow a method utilized in the past that has yielded good results, continue to try other methods as well. You may be surprised at the yield of other recruitment methods.

This Step Needs the Involvement of: The Personnel Office and Other Library Managers and Supervisors

Your personnel office and other library managers and supervisors undoubtedly will have past experience in recruiting for vacant positions. They can provide you with information on their individual past experiences.

STEP 5. IDENTIFY AND DEFINE THE POSITIVE ASPECTS OF YOUR LIBRARY AS AN EMPLOYER

Since staff recruitment is similar to marketing, to be effective you need to know your product and its potential attraction to consumers. The more thorough knowledge you have of the library, its mission, operation, staff, employee benefits, services, and the community it serves, the better prepared you'll be to "sell" the library to potential targeted applicants. Take the time to identify and draw up a list of all the facts of the library that make it a wonderful place to work, including any pertaining to salary and benefits, the work environment, and the geographic location of the work site. If there are any job-specific aspects, list those as well (see Chapter 2).

This Step Needs the Involvement of: You and, Potentially, Other Members on Staff

You can be the sole person responsible for identifying the attractive features of the library. However, the greater the spectrum of staff involved in this activity, the better. Ideally, representatives from all levels and all departments can contribute to the identification of these features.

STEP 6. RECRUIT

Now it's time to roll up your sleeves and recruit! This is your opportunity to seek out and capture the best and brightest employees for your library. It's your chance to promote your library. It's your opportunity to try various recruitment methods and refine your skills.

This Step Needs the Involvement of: All Library Staff

The greater involvement of all staff in the library's recruitment efforts, the greater the chance the library has of successfully recruiting the best employees. We tend to forget the value of team efforts in the recruitment, orientation, and long-term career development of individual employees. Existing staff should be involved in helping the library identify potential internal and external applicants for vacant positions. Each library staff member can alert potential applicants to library job opportunities.

Don't forget that all staff, as library employees, inherently serve as representatives of the library. Potential applicants may seek information from them regarding the library as an employer, the work environment, as well as the community served by the library. Every staff member—from the security guard to the janitor to the public services manager—may have an influence on whether a potential applicant ultimately submits, or fails to submit, an application for employment.

STEP 7. EVALUATE, REFINE, AND CONTINUE RECRUITING

To determine the effectiveness of your recruitment efforts and method, you need to evaluate the quantity and quality of applicants. That evaluation should be conducted in correlation to the overall staff and budgetary resources invested in the method. Based on this evaluation, refine your recruitment activities as needed. Look for ways to improve the effectiveness of your activities, and try again. Recruitment is one of those activities where the more you practice, the better you'll get at it.

This Step Needs the Involvement of: The Personnel Office

Your personnel office will be able to provide you with the statistical information needed for your evaluation, such as the number of applications received from the various recruitment sources, the number of applicants that were interviewed, the source that provided the highest number of new hires, and other factors. If they were the department responsible for implementing the recruitment, such as by placing advertisements or renting booth space, they will also be able to provide you with the actual cost of each of these activities.

2 PORTRAYING YOUR LIBRARY AS A GOOD EMPLOYER

If you regard your library as a service that needs to market its services to its community, then you realize the immediate value of promoting your library as an appealing employer. Good applicants are not hard to find, they're just hard to convince to apply for specific positions within your library unless you can demonstrate the appeal of your library as an employer. One major but often overlooked step in the recruitment process is determining those aspects of your organization that make it a desirable place to work. You'll need to be well versed in these aspects when talking to prospective applicants and should include them in your vacancy announcements and other advertisements. Let's take some time to identify the benefits of employment with your library that will draw applicants. (see Figure 2–1 for a quick review).

EIGHT WAYS TO ENHANCE COMPENSATION PACKAGES

1. REVIEW SALARY AND BENEFITS

Very few people can honestly say that money doesn't matter. Applicants do care about the salary and benefits associated with a new job. Since most of us do not have the luxury of being able to adjust salary ranges or benefit packages as desired, think about ways of positively expressing the salary and benefits of the job in comparison to others. For example, is the salary range of the position higher than comparable positions in the region, state, or nation? Or does your library offer good benefits, or benefits not commonly found in standard packages, such as long-term care, dental, or legal-services plans? Does your library offer and pay the employees' cost for life insurance, long-term disability? If so, use these as selling points.

2. IDENTIFY OTHER FORMS OF COMPENSATION

Different applicants may find other forms of compensations of equal or greater importance than salary. For instance, middle-aged appli-

---

Figure 2-1   Inventory List: What Makes Your Library a Good Place to Work?

SALARY AND BENEFITS
- Competitive salary and benefits
- Nonmonetary benefits

CAREER AND PROMOTIONAL TRACKS
- Promotional opportunities
- Training and educational opportunities
- Professional development

REPUTATION
- Of library
- Of its workers

COWORKERS
- Mentorship
- Team environment

LOCATION
- Easy access by car or public transportation
- Proximity to vacation or resort destination
- Climate
- Quality of life
- Proximity to small daily pleasures

OTHER APPEALING FEATURES

cants may place a high value on the library's retirement program. Younger applicants may prefer optional deferred-compensation programs. Know the ins and outs of these other forms of compensation. Does the library pay for all of any employee's retirement contribution, or just a percentage? After how many years is the employee vested? Or does the library offer an optional deferred-compensation (401K or 457) plan? If so, does the library match a percentage of the employee's salary in the 401K program?

3. LOOK BEYOND THE STANDARD BENEFITS PACKAGE

Not all benefits are monetary in nature. In fact, many of the most attractive benefits are not. For example, in some academic libraries one might have the option of having the summer off. Other libraries offer flexible work schedules or the ability to telecommute. Although benefits such as these may not seem attractive to everyone, they may be just the hook that brings in a quality applicant who might not otherwise have applied. Every potential applicant's life circumstance is different, so you never know what factor may offer the greatest appeal to that individual. To a single parent with young children, flexible work hours and the ability to be home when the children arrive home from school may be the biggest attraction to a new job. Or for some individuals, the ability to telecommute part-time might be the clincher. Compile a list of all these and other potential benefits available on either a library-wide or job-specific basis.

4. HIGHLIGHT PROMOTIONAL OPPORTUNITIES

One of the characteristics generally possessed by the best applicants is that they don't believe in "allowing their feet to fall asleep on the job." They tend to look for new venues that provide increased opportunities, that provide increased responsibilities, or that enhance their position. To attract these applicants, determine if your library has a good record of promotional opportunities: Does it have a reputation of promoting from within? Does it try to train and develop existing staff to move up to higher level positions? Do you have staff who started in entry-level positions who have risen through the ranks to upper management? If so, be sure to promote the opportunities for promotion or your library's reputation for promoting from within when talking to prospective applicants. This information can also be included in your general literature about the library as an employer.

5. OFFER TRAINING AND EDUCATIONAL OPPORTUNITIES

The best employees are those who can grow and adapt with the job as it evolves over time. In many circumstances, employees need training to help them stay current in their position or to excel in their job or profession. Does your library dedicate a percentage of its overall budget to staff training and development? Or does it allocate a specific training dollar amount for each member to secure training? For individuals who want to learn a specific skill, does your library provide them with training opportunities? For example, if clerical staff want to learn how to use a spreadsheet program, will your library allow or encourage them to acquire this additional skill or knowledge? Or will your library provide receptionists who have typing skills but no computer skills the opportunity to learn word processing either on the job or through formal training?

Remember that you are trying to "sell" the position and the library. Some applicants may be looking for a good place to learn new skills or methods not readily learned elsewhere. Others may want a job offering cross-training programs that will enable them to move into other areas; for example, if a cataloger is interested in moving into public services, does your library provide the training and the opportunity to staff public-help desks or reference desks? If your library does not offer cross-training programs, look into the possibility of implementing one. Such a program is good not only for recruitment purposes but also for development of existing staff as well.

6. TALK ABOUT PROFESSIONAL/PERSONAL DEVELOPMENT OPPORTUNITIES

Every library can offer professional or personal development opportunities; does yours? These opportunities can be as simple as encouraging staff to get involved in professional, community, or service organizations, and providing them with flexible schedules to do so. Toward the other end of the spectrum, the library can give employees paid leave time to participate in professional activities and support them when they hold offices in an association.

Information about professional and personal development opportunities are best promoted orally during a later stage in the recruitment process. These opportunities can be discussed after a job interview, or during the job offer stage. Although opportunities for personal and professional development are a "selling point," overall they are of lower importance than other positive aspects of a job or employer.

7. CAPITALIZE ON THE LIBRARY'S REPUTATION

Does your library have a prestigious reputation? In show business there's the eternal advice, "If you've got it, flaunt it!" It's not vanity but purely good business to promote your library's strengths to prospective applicants. Has your library earned a reputation for being innovative or creative? Does it excel in service or innovation in technology application? Will having worked in your library significantly enhance an individual's resume?

8. PROFILE COWORKERS

We all know that one's coworkers can make the job a pleasure, or a living hell. Will the successful applicant be working with respected, highly regarded coworkers? Will these coworkers serve as good mentors? Do the individuals in the unit work well as a team?

DISCOVER YOUR LIBRARY'S APPEALING FEATURES

Some of the most attractive features of a job pertain to its location. These are features that, as the saying goes, "you just can't put a price tag on."

LOCATION

Undoubtedly, some locales are more desirable than others. Stop to think if your library can be regarded as residing in a good location. For instance, is your library in or near an area that is or could be regarded as a vacation destination? Although you may not think of it as such, others may. The best way to determine if the area can be considered a vacation "destination" is by the number of visitors to the area. Is there a quantity of people who drive into the area for a day to see local sights or to partake in other area activities? Do people fly in for the weekend or longer periods for non-business-related matters? Consider factors such as:

- Is the library located in an area near a lake, ocean, or forest? Is your library within walking distance or a short drive of any of these?
- Can the area boast a sunny climate or mild winters, or exceptional air quality? The general temperatures in the area can often be a selling point. What is your climate like? Can you compare it to that of a vacation destination on the globe? What is the air quality like? Desert climates are often perfect for individuals with severe allergies. And clean, cool, crisp air may be just what asthmatics may be seeking.
- Check with your local or state department or office of tourism for additional information on the tourist attractions of your area.

RECREATION

After-hours activities are often strong draws to potential applicants. Be ready to answer questions about recreational opportunities.

- Is there convenient access to recreational activities? Since recreational activities take many forms, a good place to start is the telephone directory. How many golf courses, tennis courts, skating rinks, and swimming pools are in or near the community? Is winter skiing or summer boating accessible nearby?
- Does the community offer a variety of team sports or recreational activities? Are there local baseball, football, and other team sports open to interested individuals? Does the local recreation department or YMCA offer a walking club, or introductory golf lessons? Some local community colleges also organize a number of community recreational events.
- Does the community have continuing education or recreational classes and activities?

QUALITY OF LIFE

At some point, virtually every applicant will look at the quality of life in the area surrounding the library. The most common items to be considered by applicants are the crime rate, the quality of schools, the appropriateness of the area to raise children, and the cost of living. If the cost of living in the area is high, find out if it is comparable to the cost of living in other areas of the same size or region. Other factors to think about include the area's sense of "community," its traffic, and access to the arts and cultural events.

PROXIMITY TO SMALL PLEASURES

We often forget those little things that can help make a job pleasant. For example is there a variety of reasonably priced, good restaurants within proximity of the library? At lunch time, are there places to shop within walking distance? For those who opt to use public transportation, is it convenient in the area? For those who like driving, is there free or low-cost parking nearby?

If you're targeting and seeking to recruit applicants from the local community, you may want to put yourself in the shoes of a potential applicant to identify reasons to work for the library. At one time or another we've all contemplated how nice it would be to work close to home. Every day you could walk to work—maybe even walk or drive home for lunch or a nap! And during the work day you would be interacting or providing library services to your neighbors. There may be many more attractions to working close to the library. Don't hesitate to talk to local patrons to get input.

THE NEIGHBORHOOD

The positive aspects of your library as an employer may not be readily apparent, but every library has them. One exercise to help you get started will also give you some physical exercise as well. Take a couple of hours one afternoon and walk the neighborhood surrounding the library or branch with the job vacancy. As you stroll around, note your surroundings as if it were the first time you had ever seen them. Pay attention to the services available, such as day-care centers, schools, grocery stores, banks, accessibility to public transportation, and parking. Look for other items that may play a role in an applicant's personal life, such as churches, health clubs, and coffee shops. If the area is primarily residential, note the demographics of the area—whether it's a new neighborhood with primarily young families, or an older established neighborhood with lots of retirees around during the day. Pay attention to any desirable characteristics, such as whether there are neighborhood watches in the area, or if the homes and yards are well maintained. I'm always impressed if I walk through a neighborhood and find one or two residents out mowing lawns or tending yards during the day who smile and say hello to me or any other stranger passing by. From your observations begin creating your list of attractive features regarding the location of the library.

If you get stuck, think back to when you applied for a job in the library. Why did you want to work there? What was its initial appeal? Now that you've worked at the library for a while, what do you like best about working there on a day-to-day basis? Add these features to your list.

ADVERTISING YOUR APPEAL

Once you've identified the attractive features of the job, and of the library as an employer, include some of them in your job announcements, cover letters, and classified advertisements. You can highlight these features in a variety of ways. Below are samples of how different employers have done so:

> The monthly salary range is $4,871 to $5,897, with a minimum 3% COL increase anticipated in April. A premier benefit package includes employer-paid retirement, health (including vision and chiropractic), dental, and life insurance, 401(a) plan, cafeteria plan, overtime, tuition reimbursement plan, retiree benefits, and liberal leave benefits.

Or consider:

> CMU provides a healthcare package, life insurance, an excellent retirement program with tax-deferred investment options, tuition waiver for employee and family, paid holidays, sick leave and vacation, and competitive salaries in an environment committed to excellence and service.

Both of these examples highlight the monetary and related benefits. The first was from an advertisement from a sanitation district recruiting for a manager, and the second is from an ad recruiting for a program director at a university.

Now let's take a look at how positive factors about the location of the job can be expressed in advertisements. The first excerpt is from an ad for a position in a large metropolitan area; the second is for a job in a rural remote area.

> Amenities such as excellent schools, concert halls, sports arenas, enclosed malls, passenger rail transportation and an international airport are on par with many larger cities, yet with a "small town" atmosphere and ease of living.

> Envision yourself water skiing, sailing, or fishing on a beautiful clear lake, which features 100 miles of shoreline surrounded by gorgeous mountains. Located within the Pacific Coast mountain range, Lake County is approximately 125 miles from San Francisco, 100 miles from Sacramento, and 90 miles from the Pacific Coast.

Since most of us work in libraries that fall somewhere in between the two types of locations described in the above ads, the following are some phrases for jobs located in those "in-between" areas:

> "The area provides attractive living in a moderate climate."

> "The setting offers all the advantages of a small town with a pristine environment and a reasonable cost of living."

> "This area enjoys abundant sunshine and is within easy driving distance of excellent hiking, skiing, and water sports."

> "The cost of living is very reasonable when compared with other university communities."

> "We're located in a supportive community."

"The county is rich in historical, cultural, and educational resources."

Information on attractive features of the area can also be included in the cover letter of any vacancy notices you mail out. The proper use of these "attractions" can be very effective in grabbing the interest of readers, and can entice them to look at an enclosed job announcement. Figure 2–2 provides examples of the effective use of attractive features of the job, or the location of the library in a cover letter. In the first example, I had previously never heard of Hialeah, Florida, and was not looking for a job at the time I received the job announcement and letter. But the cover letter enticed me to read through the enclosed job notice. In the second example, the cover letter includes positive features about the position, the library environment, and the location of the library.

To recruit quality applicants effectively, you have to be an effective salesperson. Become familiar with the advantages of working at your library so that every time you speak or write about vacant positions, you automatically boast of some of these benefits. Highlight some of the benefits in every recruitment advertisement you create. Each time you talk to either potential applicants or the press, be sure to promote the positive aspects of the library as an employer.

Figure 2–2 Sample Cover Letters Containing Positive Aspects of the Library

Raul L. Martinez
Mayor

Alex Morales
Council President

Julio Robaina
Council Vice President

City of Hialeah

Council Members

Raymundo Barrios
Carmen Caldwell
Rene Garcia
Marie Rovira
Jose Yedra

City of Hialeah
John F. Kennedy Public Library
190 West 49th Street
Hialeah, Florida 33012

October 26, 1998

Dear Librarian:

Greetings from sunny South Florida!

Have you ever thought of living and working in one of the most beautiful, diverse, and multi-ethnic areas in the world? An area with a year-round tropical climate, a dynamic economy, wonderful beaches, international cuisine and a variety of cultural activities? If so, then Hialeah, Florida might just be for you! It is often said that the only two things one can't do in South Florida are go mountain climbing or snow skiing. Other than that we have it all!

Hialeah (Florida's fifth largest City) is located in South Florida, minutes from Miami and Ft. Lauderdale. Hialeah has 215,000 residents, of which 80% are Spanish speaking or bilingual. Our Spanish collection includes videos, audio books, CDs, and over 10,800 Spanish books.

Attached you will find a notice that the City of Hialeah is accepting applications for the position of Librarian I and Librarian II. If you feel that you are qualified to fill one of the challenging positions that we have available, then please send or fax your resume today.

Should you have any questions you can contact me at 305–818–9140.

Thank you.

J. Mark Taxis
Library Director
City of Hialeah

501 Palm Avenue, Hialeah, FL 33010-4789
♻ *Printed on Recycled Paper*

CITY OF SANTA ANA
20 CIVIC CENTER PLAZA • P.O. BOX 1988
SANTA ANA, CALIFORNIA 92702

SANTA ANA IS LOOKING FOR LIBRARIANS

I am pleased to announce that Santa Ana is currently hiring bilingual Librarians, with openings in the following divisions: Outreach, Adult Services, and Youth Services. The current monthly salary range is $3,052–$3,896, which reflects a recent 3.5% salary increase. In addition to salary, Santa Ana Librarians receive an additional $100 per month for bilingual assignment pay plus an excellent benefits package. Benefits include life insurance, long-term disability insurance, health and dental insurance, as well as a generous retirement plan and an optional deferred compensation plan.

Employees of Santa Ana enjoy the satisfaction of working in a total quality environment characterized by highly performing cohesive teams which are full partners in providing excellent customer service to the citizens of Santa Ana! Personal and professional growth is enhanced through a commitment to training which has been recognized by the American Society of Training and Development.

Santa Ana is located 33 miles southeast of Los Angeles, 10 miles inland from the Pacific Ocean and 90 miles north of San Diego. The City encompasses an area of approximately 27 square miles and is the ninth largest city in California and the 52nd largest in the nation. Enriched by its Hispanic history and multi-cultural environment, Santa Ana is a community active in arts and culture. This is reflected in symphonies, theaters, a municipal zoo and The Bowers Museum of Cultural Art, which has been identified as one of the nine "must see" museums in the nation.

As the county seat of Orange County, the Santa Ana civic center complex houses various government and judicial buildings. Several major institutions of higher learning serve the area, including Santa Ana Community College, the University of California Irvine and California State University, Fullerton. Easy access to five major freeways bring world-famous amusement parks and beaches to within minutes of the city.

Job announcements for each Librarian position are enclosed. Candidates must apply for each position separately. To obtain an application packet or additional announcements, please call (714) 647–5340 or write to City of Santa Ana, Personnel Services, 20 Civic Center Plaza, P.O. Box 1988, Santa Ana, CA 92702. For additional information, please feel free to contact Michael Ernandes, Personnel Operations Manager at (714) 647–5340.

Sincerely

Rob Richard
Library Director
1/99

3 DETERMINING CURRENT AND FUTURE OPENINGS

When an employee leaves or retires from the library, an employer's first thought is often to try to fill the vacancy as soon as possible. Although there may be immediate advantages to quickly filling the position, greater benefits lie in taking the time to conduct a job analysis to determine if there are some responsibilities better handled by other employees, and to decide whether the vacant position should be restructured—two critical steps in successful recruitment of high caliber staff. More importantly, you cannot effectively recruit the best applicants until you determine the exact job for which you will be evaluating them.

There are additional benefits to be derived from a job analysis, especially if the incumbent has been there for numerous years. The longer an incumbent has been in place, the greater the likelihood that the duties listed in the original job description are no longer accurate. An analysis of the position will provide you with the opportunity and data needed to alter, redesign, realign, or eliminate the position, as appropriate.

The information garnered from this process can also be used to determine the appropriate salary range for the position, based upon the level of skills and knowledge needed to perform the job. Although job analyses are most frequently conducted on positions to be vacated, they can also be performed for any position to determine if a more appropriate salary should be implemented.

UNDERSTAND THE PURPOSE OF A JOB ANALYSIS

A job analysis, also known as a job audit, enables you to examine and document the nature and responsibilities of a specific job. It helps you understand the need for the job and the specific skills and personality required to perform the job effectively so that you can write an accurate job description. The job analysis also gives you the opportunity to consider reassigning higher level responsibilities to others on staff and the lower level responsibilities to other new hires, to determine what some of the ongoing continuing education needs of the position are, and to decide whether the job should be restructured, downgraded, or possibly even eliminated.

Job analysis assists you in conveying to prospective applicants the purpose of the job and how it fits within the library or larger organization. You gain insight into the working conditions of the position, and you establish a base upon which to evaluate applicants.

When a position becomes vacant, it's easy to pull out and use the old job description to solicit applicants. But the small investment of time required to conduct a job analysis will ultimately yield a more efficient and effective work group in the long term. The process is a simple one.

CONDUCT A JOB ANALYSIS

A job analysis involves solicitation of information from the employee, job observation, and analysis. Therefore the job analysis needs to begin before an employee has vacated the position. Ideally, the employee assists in the process, unless the circumstances surrounding the employee's departure would make this counter-productive. Certain data are best obtained from the employee, yet other data are better obtained through observation.

Before you begin the analysis or determine the best method of getting the information, you need to specify what information needs to be gathered. Although this information will generally vary as a result of the position being either a professional or support position, or "blue collar" or "white collar" position, there are still basic data to obtain regardless of the type of position. The first and foremost information to acquire is a description of those tasks and duties currently performed in the position, and the percentage of time devoted to each task. The description should be brief (fewer than three sentences) but adequately portray the complexity of the duty. For example, a statement such as "time-keeping duties" is adequate, but a better description would be "maintain records of department employees' absences, the reasons for absences, and prepare a monthly report to be submitted to the personnel department."

The next type of data to identify are the responsibilities of the position. Whereas the job duties are specific tasks, the job responsibilities are much broader and subsequently more vague due to the influence of varying uncontrollable factors. For instance, a job responsibility could be staff supervision. Again, the more specific description of the responsibility the better. Listing "employee supervision" is adequate, but a better statement would be "oversees six clerical staff members who provide support to the eight professionals in the department, distributes work assignments to clerical staff, and monitors timeliness and quality of the completion of those assignments."

Once the job duties and responsibilities have been identified, then you need to detail the knowledge and skills required to successfully carry out the duties. Do applicants need a formal education or training program to carry out the job assignments? Or are special skills—such as technical skills or bilingual communication skills—necessary for them to perform the job duties effectively? For example, if one of the job responsibilities is providing microcomputer troubleshooting for the unit, education and training in microcomputer hardware and software is required.

Beyond formal education and training, try to find out what specific on-the-job training needs to be provided to the employee. If your library uses an online or other system unique to your library, is the incumbent required to know the system? Although every new employee will require some level of training and orientation to a new job, the audit must identify those skills or pieces of knowledge that can be learned *only* through training provided by your library.

The specific people with whom the employee interacts on a regular basis should be noted. For each of these individuals, list their title or position, department, organization or agency, and general frequency of contact. Next, list the general reason or purpose for the interaction. For example, if the job audited is responsible for monitoring the progress of grant-funded projects in all the branch libraries, the incumbent contacts Ms. Smith in Branch X and Mr. Doe in Branch Z on a quarterly basis to gather statistical activity reports and to identify any new problems Ms. Smith or Mr. Doe are having with the projects.

Another consideration for inclusion in the audit is whether there are any physical requirements. If the incumbent receives or distributes library mail, which often consists of large shipments of books or other materials, are there certain physical requirements for the job, such as the ability to lift a certain weight? Or is the incumbent required to be a certain height in order to shelve materials in certain locations?

Are there other special facets of the position? Is the incumbent required to work irregular or varying hours? Does the position involve frequent or extended travel? Does the incumbent have to be "on call" for any reason? These should also be noted in the audit.

During the audit, specify any special licenses or certifications that may be necessary. This could take the form of a special class of driver's license, which may be required to drive a bookmobile, or it could be a special education certification to work in a school or academic library. For your technical positions, is certification required for the operation or maintenance of telecommunication or other systems?

The audit also needs to identify any potential hazards of the job. Regardless of how staff may view it, serving on a public desk is not regarded as a job hazard, regardless of how risky it may seem from time to time! Job hazards are generally not a concern except for positions such as security guards, or those involving operation of potentially hazardous equipment or handling potentially hazardous materials. If you are auditing jobs pertaining to security, mailroom or shipping operations, or preservation, do seriously examine potential job hazards.

The considerations just discussed are generally regarded as "standard" components of a job analysis. To assist you at the job description update stage, however, it is helpful to include two additional elements in the audit. The first is how performance in the position is measured or evaluated. Is performance evaluated quantitatively, such as by the number of new serials checked in and processed, or books shelved? Or is it measured qualitatively, such as by the thoroughness and correctness of reference questions answered, or detailed level of cataloging of new materials? Or is it a combination of both methods—or some other measure of performance?

The second element is what, if any, responsibilities this position is expected to take on in the near future and why. Obtaining this information from the incumbent, the supervisor, and the section manager will be most beneficial. Find out the manager's reasoning as to the necessity of adding the responsibility, the supervisor's view of the potential pros and cons of adding the responsibility to the position, and the incumbent's view of the logic and realism of the responsibility being successfully integrated into the job.

Now you are ready to actually begin the audit process (a sample audit form can be found on page 25). The job audit can be completed by the incumbent, by the supervisor, or by the personnel department through observation and interview of the incumbent and supervisor. The most effective job audit, however, will comprise all three components. The incumbent or supervisor may have a biased or distorted view of the position being audited, and staff in the personnel office do not have the in-depth knowledge of the position that the incumbent and supervisor possess. So in the best scenario, the audit will be completed, reviewed, and merged into one document by all three participating parties.

Worksheet: Job Audit Form

Date: _____   Audit Conducted by: Name _____

Title _____

Dept./Unit_____

JOB TITLE:

DEPARTMENT UNIT:

JOB RESPONSIBILITIES:

JOB DUTIES:

Does the position involve supervision of employees?   _____ yes _____ no

If **no,** skip to Education/Training Required:

Number of employees supervised: _____

Classification of staff supervised
_____

Level of supervision provided
_____

EDUCATION/TRAINING REQUIRED:

LICENSES/CERTIFICATIONS REQUIRED:

PHYSICAL REQUIREMENTS:

SPECIAL REQUIREMENTS:

LOCAL SPECIALIZED TRAINING LIBRARY MUST PROVIDE INCUMBENT:

JOB HAZARDS:

INTERACTION WITH OTHERS:

Who: _____   Reason for Interaction: _____

METHOD OF PERFORMANCE EVALUATION:

POTENTIAL FUTURE RESPONSIBILITIES TO BE ADDED TO THE POSITION:

WRITE JOB DESCRIPTIONS

Once you've completed the job audit, you're ready to address the job description. Even though a job description already exists for the position, you can't skip over this step. Instead, consider this your opportunity to review and revise the description to better reflect the job and your personnel needs. For instance, having just completed a job analysis, you may have decided to modify the job since the last time it was filled. Or the existing job description does not accurately reflect the position's growing use and reliance on various technologies. Whatever the case, each time a position becomes vacant, the job description for that position needs to be reviewed and revised before recruitment of applicants begins.

Job descriptions serve two roles. The first is to help the recruiter solicit applicants who possess the skills and knowledge required for the job. In large organizations, the recruitment officers may or may not have a background in library operations or experience in recruiting varying levels of library staff. In such cases, the recruiter relies heavily upon the job description to gain sufficient knowledge of the nature and responsibilities of the job needed to solicit and match appropriate applicants to the position. The better the job description, the better a job the recruiter will be able to do.

The second role of job descriptions is to give applicants an overview and an understanding of the job. It should present clearly the activities, responsibilities, and function of the position within the organization so that applicants will know just what position they are applying for.

At this point, beware of falling into the trap of revising the job description based solely upon what is currently or has most recently been done in the job. The job description should be based upon the current duties of the job *and* the duties that need to be performed in the job as well—duties that may be new ones to be added to the position, or ones that were previously not included for any number of reasons.

Since books on writing job descriptions abound, we'll just briefly review the basic elements of a description from the viewpoint of the its role as a recruitment tool. The five basic elements of a job description are: (1) the job title and/or classification, (2) the job duties and responsibilities, (3) the qualifications required, (4) desirable characteristics and skills, and (5) the salary and benefits. The job title and the salary and benefit elements are the two most important recruitment components of the description. See page 25 for a worksheet that will help in completing this task.

Worksheet: Job Description

JOB TITLE:

JOB CLASSIFICATION (IF APPLICABLE):

JOB RESPONSIBILITIES:

- [arrange in order of importance]

- [responsibility]
  —[duties]

- [responsibility]
  —[duties]

- [responsibility]
  —[duties]

JOB REQUIREMENTS/QUALIFICATIONS:

- Minimum qualifications

- Desirable qualifications

SALARY/COMPENSATION:

CHOOSE APPEALING JOB TITLES

Job titles are like bait: they can lure individuals into finding out more about a vacancy. Remember, the best and the brightest individuals in any profession always have an eye out for the next job challenge or position that will assist them in their career quest. The more interesting or attractive the job title, the more likely an individual is to consider submitting an application for the position. Improving a job title is a small task that can help improve your recruitment success rate.

The job title should be descriptive and contemporary. All too frequently you'll see ads for vacancies with job titles such as library assistant or librarian. These titles are really job classifications rather than effective job titles. They indicate whether a job is at the professional or support level, but fail to convey any sense of the actual nature of the position. Librarians and library assistants may work in any number of library functions. Effective job titles reflect the job responsibilities, not the classification.

For example, you may have an opening for a position classified as librarian, but its primary responsibility is development and oversight of the library's Web site. The job title should not be librarian but rather something along the lines of "Web Designer." You have to temporarily step into the shoes of the potential applicants you're trying to recruit. If you were a fairly recent (within the last five years) MLS graduate with a heavy background in Internet Web page design, and your career interest is to move more into the management of information systems field in the computer industry, wouldn't you be more apt to take a closer look at a job advertisement for a Web designer than a librarian?

Whenever possible, stay away from one-word job titles that are nondescriptive and fairly boring. For example, the title of a position in which the librarian's primary responsibility is to be the lead person in maintaining the library's various electronic resources could be the Electronic Information Resources Librarian or Electronic Information Systems Librarian, rather than just Librarian I or II. Or the library assistant whose primary job responsibility is to staff the General Assistance Desk at the entrance to the library may hold the job title of User Services Assistant. Bear in mind that job titles and job classifications are distinct entities.

The sample titles in the box on page 29 give you an idea of some nondescriptive titles to avoid and some that really let the applicant know more about the job.

Figure 3–1   Making Job Titles Descriptive

Avoid these titles	Use these descriptive titles
Library Technician	Children's Department Assistant Copy Cataloger
Librarian	Youth Services Programming Specialist Preservation Services Librarian Web Developer Collection Development Librarian Adult Services Reference Librarian
Library Manager	Head, User Services Unit Manager of the Fairview Branch Library Community Relations Manager Assistant Head, Digital Library Production Department Children's Services Supervisor

---

In public and academic libraries you're often bound by working with civil service classifications such as Librarian I, II, III, or Assistant Librarian, Associate Librarian, or Librarian. Although these are classifications you must abide by, you do generally have the power to develop or revise a position's working title with ease. If your library does utilize certain classifications, you should use the job title in the heading of your advertisements, and include the job classification in the body of the ad.

ORGANIZE JOB RESPONSIBILITIES INTO MEANINGFUL CATEGORIES

The job description should have the job responsibilities and the related specific duties clearly delineated. The most effective arrangement of data within this category is to organize the responsibilities by their importance, with the major responsibilities listed first. Each duty or responsibility should be clearly described as much as possible. Stay away from one-word descriptions and opt for descriptive phrases. Figure 3–2 provides some tips on descriptions to avoid.

DEFINE YOUR JOB QUALIFICATIONS

Thanks to your job analysis, you have already assessed the knowledge, skills, experience, and education needed for a person to function successfully in the position. When developing this "desirable" section of the description, distinguish between the minimum job qualifications needed and the qualifications you want. Since advertisers have

Figure 3–2 Describing Job Duties and Responsibilities Adequately

Whenever possible, avoid one- or two-word descriptions of job duties, which do not adequately describe the variety or range of associated responsibilities. Instead, opt for descriptive phrases that accurately portray what the position entails.

Avoid	Better Ways to Describe the Duty
Cataloging	Use OCLC to catalog books and serials to full MARC standards.
	Perform original cataloging of archival materials and prepare MARC AMC records.
Services to children	Responsible for developing and implementing monthly story times, reading programs, and after-school activity programs for children.
	Identify and select audio-visual materials to be added to the children's collection.
Patron instruction	Instruct patrons on an individual basis, and in regularly scheduled workshops, on how to use the library's Web-based catalog and printed and electronic reference resources.
	Develop instructional materials for patrons on how to use the library's CD-ROM databases.
Supervision	Provide direct supervision of five full-time librarians (three adult reference services librarians, one young adult services librarian, and one children's services librarian).
	Direct the work of three full-time secretaries and two part-time student assistants who provide clerical support to the eight professional staff members in the unit.
Computer support	Responsible for installing both software and hardware upgrades on the department's seven staff microcomputer workstations.
	Install new Windows-based public workstations and terminals as acquired, including software and CD-ROM–networked, public access workstations.

an inclination to want to recruit staff ready to "hit the ground running," there's also the inclination to list desirable qualifications as minimum requirements. This could be to your detriment. By setting a higher level of minimum qualifications, you may minimize your applicant pool as well as eliminate applicants who meet the minimum qualifications but not necessarily the desirable qualifications. You may be depriving your library of some very outstanding individuals who could excel in the position. Consider carefully which knowledge, skills, abilities, and experience are minimum requirements, and which are simply desirable.

LIST DESIRABLE CHARACTERISTICS FOR CANDIDATES

To assist potential applicants in determining whether they may be a good candidate for a position, include desirable characteristics and skills in the job description. An applicant's characteristics and skills are often weighted equally with the applicant's experience in the final selection process. Chapter 4 addresses in detail how to determine desirable characteristics and skills of potential future employees.

INCLUDE INFORMATION ON SALARY AND BENEFITS

The importance of this section needs no explanation. Although the majority of individuals who choose to work in this field did not do so with dreams of six-digit salaries, the job salary is important to anyone who has to work for a living. Be sure to include information regarding the salary and benefits of the position in the job description.

If the salary of the position is considered low, you can make the position more attractive by including other desirable factors about the position, the library, or its location in the job description and job ad. These other "desirables," identified in the previous chapter, include pleasantries such as flexible work schedules, the option to telecommute, and other nonmonetary benefits.

As you complete the development or revision of an existing description, remember its various purposes. It provides both your recruiters and applicants with an understanding of the job. It is a tool to interest individuals in submitting an application for the position. And it also provides the library with documentation regarding the nature of the position.

Figure 3–3 contains a good example of an effective job description/ announcement. It includes information regarding the attractive features of the location of the library, the library itself, as well and the position. It also provides potential applicants with a good description of the position and its responsibilities.

Figure 3–3 Sample Job Description/Announcement

THE CITY OF FORT WORTH SEEKS A PROACTIVE, INNOVATIVE AND EXPERIENCED LIBRARIAN TO SERVE AS ITS LIBRARY DIRECTOR

Fort Worth Public Library System Serves As An Accessible And Complete Resource Center For All Citizens Of The Community.

THE CITY

The City of Fort Worth is the "western anchor" to the Dallas-Fort Worth Metroplex and has a population of 484,500 citizens with over 1.3 million people residing in Tarrant County. Tracing its roots back to early Texas history and the 1840's, the region was home to an army outpost protecting settlers (Camp Worth) and a major stop on the Chisholm Trail for cattle herds being driven to Kansas. The area's rich cultural heritage and historic past celebrate the diversity of its original Spanish explorers, Native American tribes, and related western history.

Today, Fort Worth has evolved into a community of great promise and opportunity built upon the pragmatic and hard working approach of its original citizens. The City is home to some of the country's most innovative and progressive businesses. These include the corporate offices or major facilities of Albertson's, American Airlines, Bell Helicopter, Burlington Northern/Santa Fe Railroad, Coca-Cola, Coors, FedEx, Haggar Corporation, Intel, Lockheed-Martin, Motorola, Nestles Foods, Nokia, Sprint Communications, Tandy Corporation, Union Pacific Resources, Winn Dixie, Zenith Electronics, Bass Enterprises and J.C. Penney.

Traces of its "rough and tumble past" can be found in Fort Worth's historic Stockyards District, Sundance Square, and the world's biggest honky-tonk, Billy Bob's. The focus of Fort Worth's cultural orientation is typified in the Kimball Art Museum, Modern Art Museum, Museum of Science and History, and the Amon Carter Museum, which house world-renowned art collections. The Fort Worth Symphony Association, Opera Association, Ballet and Van Cliburn International Piano competition host internationally recognized talents. For sports enthusiasts, a wide range of professional and semi-professional sports teams are nearby to accompany the region's extensive parks and recreation system and deluxe sports facilities such as Gateway Park, the Haws Athletic Center, and the Texas Motor Speedway. Professional Football, Baseball, Basketball and Hockey are available in nearby cities. Fort Worth is the home of two semi-professional hockey teams.

The Fort Worth Independent School District Board of Education was recognized

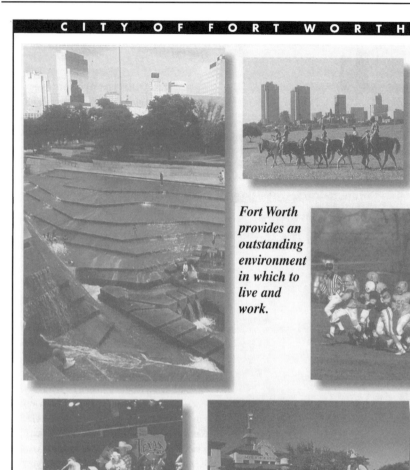

CITY OF FORT WORTH • TEXAS

Fort Worth provides an outstanding environment in which to live and work.

as having one of the most effective boards of education in the nation, according to the ABC-TV news feature "American Agenda". Several well-recognized institutions of higher education are within easy driving distance or located within the community. Texas Christian University (TCU), Tarrant County Junior College (TCJC), Brite Divinity School, Texas Wesleyan University, University of North Texas Health Science Center and Wesleyan School of Law are located within Fort Worth. The University of Texas has a major campus in neighboring Arlington. The University of North Texas and Texas Woman's University are also located in nearby Denton. Southern Methodist University and various campuses of the University of Dallas are within easy reach in Dallas, as well.

The DFW Metroplex is one of the largest consumer and industrial markets in the U.S. with a total population in excess of five million. Fort Worth was awarded "All America City" status in 1993 by the National Civic League. The award was in recognition of the City's innovative approaches for including citizens in strategic planning processes and for its practical problem-solving efforts regarding urban issues. Fort Worth provides an outstanding environment in which to live and work.

CITY GOVERNMENT

Fort Worth functions under the Council-Manager form of government. The nine-member City Council is elected for two-year concurrent terms. The Mayor is elected at large and the eight Council Members are elected from Single Member Districts. The

City Manager is one of the Council appointees in conformance with the City Charter and is responsible for the day-to-day operations of municipal government. The City Manager serves at the pleasure of the City Council. Four Assistant City Managers provide support to the City Manager. Fort Worth operates with a total of over 5,200 employees and an overall budget of $560 million.

POSITION OVERVIEW

Under the specific direction and guidance of the City Manager and Assistant City Manager, the Library Director assists in the formulation and recommendation of organizational strategies, objectives, policies and programs in support of the City Council. The Director is responsible for providing effective leadership and direction to the public library system while ensuring effective/efficient utilization of employees, funds, materials, facilities and time. The Director is responsible for implementing city policies/procedures and the timely reporting in the progress of projects or goals and decisions determined by the City Manager's Office. Specifically, the Library Director:

• Guides and is responsible for the day-to-day administration and operation of the Fort Worth Public Library System (FWPLS) in compliance with appropriate laws and regulations, accepted administrative management principles and within technical guidelines accepted by the American and Texas State Library Associations.

• Prepares an annual budget and submits it for review to the City Manager's Office. The Director is responsible for ensuring proper budgetary/fiscal administration in addition to monitoring and maintaining the financial integrity of the system.

• The Director serves as primary coordinator for technical resources to the City Manager's Office, Library Advisory Board members and acts as an advisor on formulation of programs to monitor and improve services to the general public.

• As directed by the City Manager's Office, assumes an active liaison role between various federal, state and regional organizations, professional associations, civic groups and private citizens and enterprises, the media and various regulatory bodies. The Director will serve as spokesperson

The $6.7 million reconstruction of the Central Library, cornerstone of the Fort Worth Public Library System, is almost completed.

to a wide variety of groups and will make presentations to the City Council or external groups as necessary.

• Contributes to the effective administration of the agency by fostering an attitude among staff, which encourages cooperation, coordination of efforts, efficient/intelligent use of resources and a service orientation toward the public.

• Provides policy and strategic options for the City Manager's Office and assists in the development of long-range plans for the FWPLS' required functions. Carries

out the policy directives and organizes activities to enhance Fort Worth's abilities to meet its goals and objectives.

• Establishes and reviews service and general performance standards for the system, conferring with subordinates to maximize efficiency, minimize conflicts/grievances and discrepancies in both operational and human resource areas (Affirmative Action/EEO compliance, compensation, benefits, etc.) Reports regularly to the Assistant City Manager on programs that affect the welfare of the agency.

The Director oversees a library system staffed by 177 full-time employees and which operates on an $8.9 million budget. The FWPLS consists of a central library, nine branches, two regional libraries and two

satellite facilities located in the Caville and Butler Housing Projects. The FWPLS is further supported by active organizations such as Friends of the Fort Worth Library (600 members) and the Fort Worth Public Library Foundation (7,500 contributors), as well as an active volunteer group which contributed over 27,000 hours of service; this represented a cost savings of over $175,500 for the City in 1997.

The FWPLS has over 2.08 million library materials and served almost 1.9 million users in the past year. Circulation is estimated at 4.3 million and over 1.8 million requests for information and assistance were processed via telephone, fax, Internet and dial-in access. In 1997, the first phase of the Central Library reconstruction project was 90% completed and the Library Foundation raised $4.5 million of the $6.7 million needed for the full project. The annual book budget is currently approximated at $1.4 million.

Major initiatives in capital construction, automated systems, Total Quality (TQ)/ customer service efforts and new public education/information programs will take place in 1998-1999. The nine-member Library Advisory Board may direct other priority programs or points of emphasis for the new Director in the coming year. This recruitment represents a replacement for a highly regarded and active Director/Librarian who served the FWPLS for seventeen years before announcing her retirement in early, 1998.

CURRENT ISSUES

The following issues were developed after discussions with the City Manager, Assistant City Managers, the Chair of the Library Foundation, Chair and Vice Chair of Friends of the Library, several Council members and key management team members reporting to the Library Director. Additional insights were obtained from representatives of the Library's All Staff Association and selected Department Directors within the City of Fort Worth. The issues expressed are not designed to establish fixed management priorities, but are intended to represent the types of projects and programs that a new Director will encounter in her/his first six to twelve months of employment.

Capital Construction Programs

The new Director will arrive at a critical period of time when completion of the final phases of reconstruction for the Central Library will be taking place. The Director will be asked to ensure the timely analysis on the quality of construction at the Central Library and help guide the further renovation of Branch Libraries (currently scheduled for two branches per year). Continued coordination with the Library Foundation for development of additional funds/grants/gifts to improve the physical plant(s) will be a strong focus for the new Director. In the last two years a new Regional Facility (East) has been built ($5 million). The Director must become totally familiar with the terms of design and construction contracts and develop

a strong level of support for passage of the capital programs needed to upgrade the facilities in the FWPLS. The Northside and Seminary South Branch Libraries are slated for renovation during 1998.

Automated Systems Enhancement

There is unanimous agreement that the new Director must lead the FWPLS into a new integrated technology system that will serve as part of a Five Year Strategic or Information Technology Master Plan (ITMP). Upgrade of the Dynix system and installation of a newer operating network for the Ameritech System are high priorities for the ITMP. All facilities in the system must have upgraded capacity to accommodate electronic data transmission and full computer installation/integration within FWPLS' Wide Area Network (WAN). The new Director will be expected to adopt a global outlook on the utilization of new technologies and secure the "game plan" and funding for training senior staff in the best use of technology. Part of the ITMP should also address integration of systems with local colleges/ universities, businesses and the Fort Worth Independent School District for ease of access, coordination and mutual support. Open access by the citizens to on-line services will require a strong planning effort and cost/ benefit analysis for any future automation initiatives.

Internal Relations Efforts

Because of financial and operational restrictions in the late 80's/early 90's, staff growth and development programs have been somewhat restricted. The new Director will be asked to prepare and present comprehensive and focused analysis of needs in the following areas:

• Development/funding plans for continued staff education, training and professional affiliations.

• Formalized supervisory training and use of goal oriented evaluation and team building efforts to promote independent decision making and succession planning.

• Stronger programs and efforts to establish and maintain effective working relationships with multi-cultural communities, citizen groups and supporting institutions such as FWISD, Tarrant County Junior

College, Texas Christian University, Texas Wesleyan and other colleges/universities.

The new Director must also concentrate on improving levels and frequency of communications with City Administration, the City Council, the business community and other private sources. It is imperative that the FWPLS be fully integrated into the City's organizational structure/culture as opposed to remaining "independent or different in nature." This will be necessary to attract stronger levels of commitment on major policy decisions and greater levels of financial support.

General Improvements/Issues

The new Director will be asked to develop effective approaches along a wide spectrum of issues. Briefly stated, some of the more pertinent issues for consideration include, but are not limited to:

• Special Collections/Programs – Fort Worth has a nationwide reputation for its Genealogy and English/Second Language Programs. Additional emphasis is needed to maintain those efforts and establish several other collections and programs such as ethnic collections (African American, Hispanic, Native American) and programs for persons with developmental disabilities. Upgrade of Summer Reading and Remedial Reading Programs might be included in this effort.

• Staffing Levels – Hours of Operation – The new Director should revisit and analyze re-establishing extended hours of operation/ Sunday operations for convenience to citizens/users. Accurate cost/benefit analysis must be conducted to ensure proper staffing levels and budgetary considerations.

• Employee Relations – There is a predictable level of anxiety over recruitment of a new Director after 17 years of continuity. The new Director must quickly establish herself/ himself as an open communicator, approachable and a reasonable risk taker "willing to allow employees to try new ideas". At the same time, the Director must also be a strong proponent for diversity in the workplace and sustain the excellent results recently made in having the work force reflect/mirror the make-up of the community.

CITY OF FORT WORTH • TEXAS

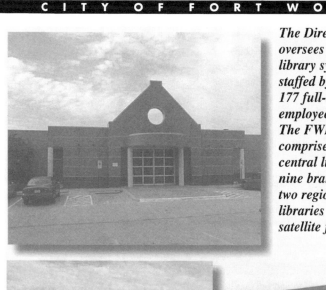

The Director oversees a library system staffed by 177 full-time employees. The FWPLS is comprised of a central library, nine branches, two regional libraries and two satellite facilities.

EXPERIENCE AND EDUCATION

The Library Director should have seven to ten years senior management experience with an emphasis on directing a multi-branch system in a large urban or suburban environment. At least five years experience in an executive position is desired. Experience working in a public/municipal library system is desired. Emphasis in background will be placed on the management skills, although sound technical orientation cannot be discounted. The new Director should have experience managing a budget and staff of reasonably comparable size or have been an Assistant/Associate Director in a larger system. While "non-traditional backgrounds" will be considered, it is generally expected that final candidates will have earned a Master's in Library Sciences from an ALA accredited university or, possess an MPA and have worked within related disciplines.

A demonstrated background in automation of library systems, review and planning for capital expansion programs and strategic planning/analysis is needed. Proven experience and participation in public/community relations programs is also required. It is essential that the selected candidate have strong financial management, administrative and organizational skills while managing an agency through a decentralized staff. The position requires experience and an interest in creating strong staff development programs while building a creative/dynamic organization. Creation of service orientation programs and philosophies should also be demonstrated.

CANDIDATE PROFILE

The selected candidate will display superior leadership skills and have a style that promotes confidence in their decision-making. The Director must be a self-motivated individual capable of developing and implementing long-range strategies in a complex municipal agency. The ability to develop cooperative working relationships among individuals with differing philosophies and priorities will be necessary. The Director must be sensitive and realistic in the development and presentation of proposals recognizing prevailing attitudes, political realities and fiscal constraints. The Director must be a poised, articulate individual, capable of communicating effectively with citizen groups, elected officials and senior management personnel. The ability to relate to citizens at all levels of the public, business and governmental entities is essential. The new Director must have the ability to motivate subordinates to deliver high quality service while striving to satisfy patron needs. The successful person will be a catalyst for action, organized, thorough in approach and capable of showing flexibility to arrive at solutions that will benefit a wide variety of the community. The person must have the stamina and interest in working until problems are solved.

While the person will oftentimes be at the center of activity, he/she must be able to work effectively behind the scenes, leaving substantial recognition to the volunteers and subordinate staff. The individual must be able to withstand criticism calmly and be able to function under tight schedules or deadlines. The successful candidate will have a positive and enthusiastic outlook toward solving complex situations.

The Director's value systems must also display honesty, integrity, ethics and acceptable social behavior as primary traits. The new Director should have a significant record and commitment in producing results in the areas of Affirmative Action/Equal Opportunity Employment. The individual must possess skills to encourage employees to advance themselves technically, plus contribute open and constructive commentary toward the successful mission of the Fort Worth Public

Library System. Strong sensitivity to issues affecting women and minorities must be evident, as well as stressing a commitment to sharing those values with the organization.

COMPENSATION

Starting salary to the high $80's – low $90's plus car allowance. An outstanding program of benefits and allowances also await the successful candidate. The opportunity to join a dynamic organization with an excellent reputation will offer long-term personal and professional growth.

APPLICATION AND SELECTION PROCESS

For additional information regarding this position, please contact:

Mr. Jerrold Oldani at:

THE OLDANI GROUP, Inc.

188 –106th Avenue NE, Suite 420
Bellevue, Washington 98004
Phone: 425.451.3938 / Fax: 425.453.6786
E-mail: searches@theoldanigroup.com

http://www.theoldanigroup.com

The final filing date is **July 13, 1998.** To be considered for the position, please submit a résumé to The Oldani Group. Following the filing date, résumés will be screened in relation to the criteria outlined in this brochure. Candidates with relevant qualifications will be given preliminary interviews by the consultant. Interviews will be followed by reference checks after receiving the candidates' permission. Candidates deemed qualified will be referred to the City of Fort Worth. A final interview process will then be scheduled for selected candidates and an eligibility list will be established in mid to late August, 1998. Texas Public Disclosure laws may allow for release of candidate name at any stage of the process; however, we will endeavor to maintain confidentiality.

The City of Fort Worth, Texas is an Affirmative Action/Equal Opportunity Employer and values diversity at all levels of its workforce.

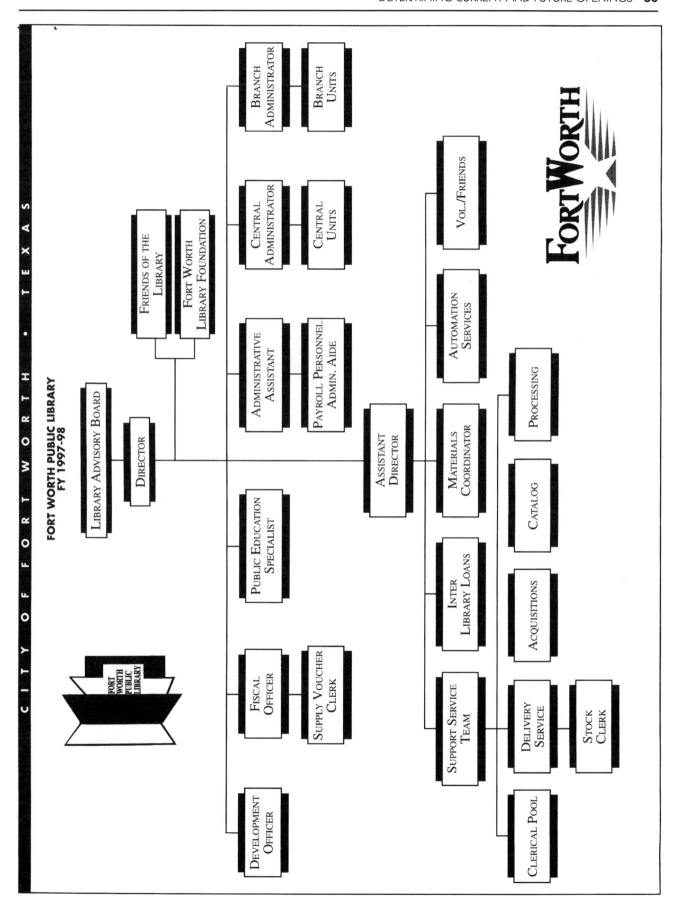

CITY OF FORT WORTH • TEXAS

FORT WORTH PUBLIC LIBRARY
FY 1997-98

FORT WORTH PUBLIC LIBRARY

LIBRARY ADVISORY BOARD

DIRECTOR

FRIENDS OF THE LIBRARY

FORT WORTH LIBRARY FOUNDATION

BRANCH ADMINISTRATOR

BRANCH UNITS

CENTRAL ADMINISTRATOR

CENTRAL UNITS

ADMINISTRATIVE ASSISTANT

PAYROLL PERSONNEL ADMIN. AIDE

DEVELOPMENT OFFICER

FISCAL OFFICER

SUPPLY VOUCHER CLERK

PUBLIC EDUCATION SPECIALIST

ASSISTANT DIRECTOR

VOL./FRIENDS

AUTOMATION SERVICES

MATERIALS COORDINATOR

INTER LIBRARY LOANS

SUPPORT SERVICE TEAM

PROCESSING

CATALOG

ACQUISITIONS

DELIVERY SERVICE

STOCK CLERK

CLERICAL POOL

FortWorth

4 DETERMINING THE GENERAL SKILLS AND CHARACTERISTICS OF INDIVIDUALS YOU SEEK TO RECRUIT

Dorothy Gale wasn't a librarian, but we can all learn from her experiences in Oz. She recognized the value of the courage of the Lion, the intelligence of the Scarecrow, and the heart of the Tin Man, as well as their willingness to take chances to reach their individual goals. If she had failed to recruit the aid of the three, she would have perished long before reaching the Emerald City. The characteristics possessed by this trio of recruits are some of those also looked for by employers. But the Scarecrow, the Tin Man, and the Lion possessed other skills and experiences that made them invaluable in Dorothy's situation—and in order for you to recruit outstanding staff, you need to identify those extra skills and characteristics that are invaluable to your library. Doing so will also help in the development of your overall recruitment program. In later chapters, we will cover how to develop recruitment advertisements and determine the best selection methods for your library, and you'll see the role this information plays in the two processes. But for now, let's focus on desirable staff characteristics.

The characteristics possessed by potential applicants are as, if not more, important than the knowledge and experience they possess. Imagine for a moment you had two applicants, one meeting the minimum qualifications and the other far exceeding them. The applicant meeting the minimum qualifications was amiable and enthusiastic about work. However, the other candidate was rude, informed you he thought supervisors are a pain in the neck, and was only interested in doing the minimum amount of work required to receive his paycheck. In this instance, would you base your final selection upon each candidate's experience and qualifications, or upon the characteristics they possess?

IDENTIFY DESIRABLE CHARACTERISTICS

Determining the characteristics you want in new employees is a painless task. To start, quickly review the conditions and environment. Will the employee be working in a team-based environment or on team-based projects? If so, look for a team player. Or if the employee is expected to work independently, the ability to work with little supervision is a plus. Are there other desireable individual characteristics based upon the specific work environment?

Next, analyze those characteristics that you want to see in all of your employees. Take some time to think about your best employees, past and present. What attributes do they possess? You should always look for employees who have the potential to be even better than the best individuals on staff. To help you get started with your list of attributes, look at Figures 4–1 and 4–2 for a sample list of characteristics and skills frequently appearing in job announcements and advertisements.

For each position, develop a list of the attributes you would like the new employee to possess. As you compile this list, also think about what characteristics new employees will need to have for future success in the job and in the library. Think about those changes or new programs or services you would like to see occur, and the characteristics an individual would need to have to be able to bring about these

---

Figure 4–1 Sample Checklist of Desirable Characteristics

Dedicated. Do you want an individual who will perform at the highest level possible, who wants to do the best job?

Reliable. Can you trust the individual to perform adequately and complete assigned tasks?

Efficient. Is efficiency essential in the individual you hire?

Detail oriented. Do you need an individual who pays attention to small matters as needed?

Consensus builder. Are there frequent situations when the individual hired will need to bring several people to general agreement on various matters?

Innovative. Are you looking for an individual who will bring new ideas, methods, or practices to the library?

Visionary. Do you seek someone who can look to the future?

Enthusiastic. Do you want an individual with intense interest in the work?

Flexible. How flexible does an individual need to be both in the specific position and in order to grow with library?

Independent worker. Would an independent worker be an asset or a detriment in the vacant position?

Team player. Is a team player needed or not needed?

Outgoing personality. If the individual hired will be working with the public or individuals outside of his department, would an outgoing personality be an asset?

changes. Do not set any limits on your list. Once you've completed your list, prioritize it so that when you write the job description and advertisements you'll know which characteristics to emphasize.

IDENTIFY DESIRABLE SKILLS AND ABILITIES

Prepare a list that includes both the general skills you want in all your library employees, and skills preferred for specific positions. It's important to take the time to put together a worksheet of desired characteristics and skills for several reasons. To successfully recruit the best applicant, you need to know everything possible about what that applicant should be. You need to select recruitment methods which will effectively reach individuals with the desired characteristics and skills. And you can't develop effective recruitment advertising without sufficient information about your target audience.

The box gives some of the more commonly desired skills and abilities for you to think about for your vacant positions. Once you've prepared your list, prioritize the skills and abilities, placing those that are mandatory at the top of the list. For your mandatory skills, identify the means by which the presence of those specific skills or abilities can be verified in applicants. If you have no means or do not intend to verify the applicants' possession of specific skills, designate those skills as desirable instead of mandatory. See page 45 for a sample worksheet to get you started.

Sample Checklist for Desirable Skills

Interpersonal skills. Does the individual need to be able to interact effectively and comfortably with others?

Written communication skills. Will the individual need to communicate effectively with others via memorandums, letters, and other written documents?

Oral communication skills. Will the individual need to communicate effectively orally with both internal and external individuals at all levels?

Listening skills. Should the individual be able to listen and understand information orally communicated to him or her before immediately responding?

Analytical skills. Does the individual need to be able to analyze various situations, problems, or projects and develop a recommendation?

Problem-solving skills. Will the individual need to evaluate problems and develop solutions?

Decision-making skills. Does the individual need to make timely decisions?

Organizational skills. Does the position require an individual with strong organizational skills at various levels?

Planning skills. Will the person be required to plan new services, programs, or facilities?

Leadership skills. Will the individual be serving in either a formal or informal leadership capacity?

Management skills. Will the successful applicant be required to manage people or projects in a timely fashion?

Supervision skills. Is the position supervisory?

Ability to work under stress. On a regular or irregular basis, will the library need to rely upon the individual to perform efficiently and effectively under stress?

Reference skills. Will the individual be called upon to provide reference assistance on a regular or irregular basis?

Training skills. Will the individual be expected to provide formal or informal one-on-one or group training for staff or patrons?

As you go through this process, keep in mind that your ultimate goal is to hire and retain the best employees. The recruiting, hiring, and training of new employees is costly. Hence, you want new employees to remain with the library for several years. Now go back and review your list of mandatory and desirable characteristics and skills, keeping an eye to the structure and environment the individual will be working in on a day-to-day basis. Will an individual with these skills and characteristics be able to work successfully and assist the library in fulfilling its mission? Or will an individual with those attributes be a "mismatch" for the organization? There's nothing sacred about your list, so be willing to adjust it as necessary to assure a "win-win" recruitment situation.

It's easy to develop a list of the characteristics and skills of an ideal applicant. Attributes such as innovative and risk taker are positive attributes—if utilized appropriately. Valued by many employers, these same characteristics, however, often send a chill down the spine of certain supervisors. For individuals with these and similar attributes,

Worksheet: Skills And Characteristics

POSITION:

DESIRED CHARACTERISTICS:
(Rank the top 10, with 1 being the most desirable).

Ranking	Characteristic	Ranking	General Skills
_____	Reliable	_____	Written communication skills
_____	Efficient	_____	Oral communication skills
_____	Detail oriented	_____	Interpersonal skills
_____	Enthusiastic	_____	Listening skills
_____	Dedicated	_____	Analytical skills
_____	Innovative	_____	Problem-solving skills
_____	Visionary	_____	Organizational skills
_____	Flexible	_____	Planning skills
_____	Team player	_____	Leadership skills
_____	Consensus builder	_____	Decision-making skills
_____	_____	_____	_____
_____	_____	_____	_____
_____	_____	_____	_____
_____	_____	_____	_____
_____	_____	_____	_____
_____	_____	_____	_____
_____	_____	_____	_____
_____	_____	_____	_____
_____	_____	_____	_____

their growth and on-the-job success hinges upon their supervisor's ability to nurture and channel those attributes to the benefit of the library. So if you are interested in recruiting individuals with these characteristics, make sure they will be placed in an environment that will foster success both for the employee and the library.

VERIFY SPECIFIC SKILLS AND CHARACTERISTICS

You can assess whether applicants possess specific skills or characteristics through two methods: the interview and reference checks. The interview process allows you to verify the presence of certain skills, such as oral communication and listening. Various interview questions can test for innovative thinking and vision, and hypothetical situation questions can help you verify analytical, problem-solving, and other related skills.

As a rule of thumb, the more references you check, the better. Prior to checking references, prepare a set of questions designed to help you obtain any specific information regarding the applicant. If the applicant is seeking a supervisory position, don't hesitate to ask for the name of a reference of a person supervised by the applicant.

KNOW THE RELEVANT LEGISLATION

Be sure to familiarize yourself with these and other relevant laws:

- Americans with Disabilities Act
  U.S. Code, Title 42, Chapter 26
  The following appears in Section 12112(a):

  No covered entity shall discriminate against a qualified individual with a disability because of the disability of such individuals in regard to job application procedures, the hiring, advancement, or discharge of employees, employee compensation, job training, and other terms, conditions, and privileges of employment.

- Age Discrimination in Employment Act
  U.S. Code, Title 29, Chapter 14
  The following appears in Section 623(a):

  It shall be unlawful for an employer—
  (1) to fail or refuse to hire or to discharge any individual or otherwise discriminate against any individual with respect to his compensation, terms, conditions, or privileges of employment, because of such individual's age;
  (2) to limit, segregate, or classify his employees in any way which would deprive or tend to deprive any individual of employment opportunities or otherwise adversely affect his status as an employee, because of such individual's age, or
  (3) to reduce the wage rate of any employee in order to comply with this chapter.

- Civil Rights Act
  U.S. Code, Title 42
  The following appears in Section 2000e-2:

  It shall be unlawful employment practice for an employer—
  (1) to fail or refuse to hire or to discharge any individual, or otherwise discriminate against any individual with respect to his compensation, terms, conditions, or privileges of employment, because of such individual's race, color, religion, sex, or national origin; or
  (2) to limit, segregate, or classify his employees or applicants for employment in any way which would deprive or tend to deprive any individual of employment opportunities or otherwise adversely affect his status as an employee, because of such individual's race, color, religion, sex, or national origin.

5 SELECTING THE LIBRARY IMAGE YOU WISH TO PROMOTE

RECOGNIZE THE IMPORTANCE OF IMAGE

A library's image plays a very important role in the recruitment process. Different types of images attract different types of applicants. Innovative libraries attract creative and innovative people, reputable research organizations attract research-oriented people, and community-oriented public libraries attract individuals who like to work with and reach out to various segments of the community. Look at the advertisements of many successful companies, and you'll see that each has its own image or identity. Just take a moment to think about companies like Apple Computers or LucasFilms, or libraries like the New York Public Library or Harvard University Library. Each has an image or identity that immediately comes to mind. Such images can attract applicants to those employers. However, negative images can also drive away potential applicants from your library. Often, especially if you are a corporate, special, or academic library, your library's image and identity may be tied to or overshadowed by your corporation's or institution's image.

DISCOVER YOUR LIBRARY'S CURRENT IMAGE

Before you embark on developing your recruitment advertising, first determine the image people have of your library. If it's negative, you need to work to overcome that. Then your library needs to define the image it wishes to promote. Let's address the first task.

To find out what your library's image is, you need to seek input from the audience served by the library, and from the library's peers. Start by determining how you will seek input from your audience. This could take the form of a questionnaire, which can easily be distributed widely through various mechanisms such as the mail or the

Internet, or by conducting telephone interviews. The questionnaire should ask respondents their perceptions of various aspects of the library, including the service and services provided, the library's collection and access to additional information, the value of the library in meeting their needs, the overall quality of staff, as well of their perception of the library as a potential employer. Your challenge is to encourage a high return rate. You may want to offer prizes to winners drawn randomly from completed questionnaires as an encouragement to return the completed survey. The main disadvantage of utilizing questionnaires is that it requires staff resources to handle the distribution, receipt, and analysis of the data.

Two other methods to consider for seeking information on your library's image are interviews with selected members of your audience, and community forums. You, or your staff, could select to survey only a small group of individuals representative of your audience as to their perceptions of the library. Or you could advertise, and hold a number of short, staff-guided discussion groups, to seek input from your audience as to your image. The one problem with such forums is that unless they are designed as part of another library event, the attendance could be very sparse.

An alternative method to community forums is to utilize focus groups. Focus groups are small groups of individuals of usually no more than ten people who are brought together for facilitated discussion on various topics. Focus groups are generally more successful than community forums for several reasons. Because a select group of individuals are selected and invited to participate, you generally have a higher rate of attendance. And with focus groups, you have the ability to find the image that specific target groups have of the library. For instance, a focus group consisting of students can give you feedback on how they perceive the library. A focus group consisting of people in their twenties will provide you with information on the image this segment has of the library.

Your next step is to determine what perception the library community has of your organization. This is important, since you will be targeting individuals who are currently employed at other libraries. Again, you can solicit this data through the same methods previously mentioned (surveys, selected interviews, and focus groups).

BE OPEN TO CHANGING THAT IMAGE

Several factors can impact the image your library currently holds. These factors range from recent library public relations campaigns, public relations and other library literature previously issued, as well as the quality and quantity of the services and materials provided. Staff interaction, and lack of staff interaction, with your client group will also greatly impact how individuals perceive the library. Every person working in the library, from the security guard at the entrance to the student aides shelving books, are considered to be library staff by your clientele, and should be provided with customer-service training as appropriate. Lack of staff interaction can also incur a potential negative view of the library—it can be annoying to plow through an automated telephone answering system and maneuver through several menus simply to ask a quick question.

Hopefully, the data you gather show both your client group and the library community have a positive image of your library. If the images are positive, are they similar? And are the images ones upon which you want to build your recruitment advertising? If the images are not positive, you need to take a break from this book to work with your library administration to develop ways to change that negative image (see Figure 5–1 for an overall strategy). You may want to consult Suzanne Walters's book *Customer Service* (1994) for tips on improving the customer service provided by the library. Whatever course your library takes, improvement of the library's image is critical to effective staff recruitment. Trying to recruit outstanding staff to work in a library with a very bad image is like a lion trying to attract deer to its den. Figure 5–2 includes tips on how to enhance your library's image from Lisa Wolfe's book *Library Public Relations, Promotions, and Communications* (1997).

Figure 5–1 Steps for Determining and Selecting the Image of the Library You Wish to Promote

1. Find out how your library audience and the library community currently perceive your library.
2. Conduct a survey, focus groups, or selected interviews to gather this information.
3. See if the image is negative; if so, work with your public relations people and library administration to change that image.
4. If the image is positive, but you wish to promote another image, select the new image in cooperation with your public relations people and library administration. The new image you select to promote should be positive, and an accurate reflection of the library as a whole, or some aspect of the library.
5. Promote that new image in all your library publications, communications, and promotions. Don't limit promotion of that image just to your recruitment materials.
6. Actively promote the new image for a minimum of several years. It takes that long for it to be effective.

Figure 5–2 Seven Tips on Enhancing Your Library's Image

1. Develop a corporate identity for your library. By developing a graphic entity or look for your library, you are working to create a particular public perception of the library.
2. Develop a clear, concise, and consistent message about the library. Make sure the message you communicate is reflected in the library's culture and policies. Creating and promoting a misleading or inaccurate message can damage your credibility.
3. Create effective print communications that promote a positive perception of the library—that get across your message about the library. These print communications can include newsletters, brochures, annual reports, flyers, posters, and bookmarks.
4. Use current technology, such as the Internet, to communicate your message about the library.
5. Develop effective relationships with the media (reporters, editors, and photographers) that enable them to get their stories, and you to tell yours. Tools you can use to encourage media coverage include news releases, news conferences, press kits, broadcast, fax, e-mail, and letters to the editor.
6. Use volunteers to help you convey the library's message. Volunteers are local representatives who can take your message back into the community. You can also develop a volunteer speaker's bureau.
7. Develop and use special programs and events to either directly communicate or assist you in communicating your message.

Lisa Wolfe, *Library Public Relations, Promotions, and Communications* (New York: Neal-Schuman, 1997).

If the image your library currently holds is one upon which you wish to build your recruitment advertising, then you should move on to the next chapter at this point. If it is not, meet with your public relations staff and library administration to discuss the image you wish to promote. Since you must be careful about not promoting conflicting library images within various units of your library, both your public relations staff and library administration need to be involved.

Remember to select an image that not only reflects a positive aspect of the library but also abets your recruitment efforts. You want to draw a select cadre of applicants to your library. Be sure that the image accurately reflects the library as a whole, or some aspect of the library. You don't want to promote a misleading or inaccurate image of the library; this could result in an enormous waste of time and staff resources. You don't want to solicit and try to fit a bunch of square pegs into round holes.

PROMOTE A POSITIVE IMAGE

Once you've identified and selected the image you wish to promote, use it in your recruitment advertising and all your recruitment and other library materials. Promote it frequently and widely—on your Web site, your library's information brochures, your bookmarks, and your library stationery. Your image should be promoted for at least several years to be effective.

PROMOTE A POSITIVE IMAGE AMONG APPLICANTS FOR PROFESSIONAL POSITIONS

Up to now, the focus has been on creating a positive image of the library within the community, since most applicants for nonprofessional and paraprofessional library positions are drawn from the local geographic regions. However, professional job vacancies usually necessitate drawing applicants from across the state or nation. Promoting a positive image of the library as an employer among potential professional applicants is vital, yet more difficult because it ties into the library's overall staff development program. And in most cases, administration of these programs is beyond the purview of the individuals responsible for staff recruitment.

The best method for promoting a positive image of the library among professional library applicants is by placing the library's best employees in highly visible situations. Your best employees are your best emissaries. Encourage them to participate actively in professional associations and to present papers at conferences that will enable them to showcase the library or its programs and services. They are living examples of your library's staff development program and your library's culture. Those old sayings about people fleeing from sinking ships and being drawn to winners hold true in recruiting. Potential applicants want to join what they perceive as being a winning team.

Another way to create a positive image among potential professional applicants is through an ongoing effort of the library to increase its visibility in the library literature. The library should continuously promote itself in the library journals through press releases regarding new or innovative services or programs. The library can also encourage its staff to submit articles about any innovative or interesting new library programs or services to the professional journals. Libraries frequently appearing in the literature for positive reasons are more apt to draw a larger and better pool of applicants than those with little name recognition.

6 USING THE BEST RECRUITMENT METHODS

Now it's time to start recruiting the best applicants. At this point you have several recruitment method options from which to choose, depending upon your needs and other factors such as the applicant pool, your recruitment resources, whether you are the sole person in charge of recruitment, and your energy level. So let's take a quick look at some of these methods; we will examine them in detail in subsequent chapters.

RECRUITMENT METHODS THAT WORK

ADVERTISE

The most common method of finding applicants, and a basic component of employee recruitment, is advertising. Advertising is a wonderful method because of its flexibility. It can accommodate any budget, big or small, and is effective whether you're a novice or an old pro at it. And you have a wide range of advertising mediums you can opt to utilize. Newspapers, professional journals, the Internet, and radio are just a few of the advertising media at your disposal. Chapter 7 takes a closer look at advertising.

RECRUIT ON CAMPUS

Recruiting on campus can be highly effective in reaching certain applicants. If you're looking for individuals with college degrees, vocational training, or to start out in entry-level positions, colleges and vocational or trade schools are a great place to begin. In addition to hosting job or career fairs, these educational institutions also contain job-placement centers and services for their students. Some colleges will even prescreen applicants for employers.

When considering on-campus recruiting, don't think of it as useful only when looking for recent college graduates. Many colleges and vocational schools also serve alumni, so you could conceivably contact highly experienced individuals. This is also an excellent way to recruit for those student aide or assistant positions. Don't overlook the local high schools as sources of applicants.

Most colleges and universities offer on-site interview facilities to employers for only a small fee. Contact the career center of the colleges in your area, or those offering the desired degrees or training programs you are looking for, to discuss the services they provide to students and employers and any associated fees.

EXHIBIT AT JOB FAIRS AND EVENTS

Announcements of job vacancies can be widely distributed through various events. Participation in job fairs and events can yield applications for vacant positions while raising the visibility of the library in the community or college. There are three basic types of job fairs and events: college job/career fairs, commercially sponsored job fairs, and community job fairs.

In general, colleges hold at least one annual job/career event on campus, which is usually a one-day event. Although some colleges do not charge employers any fees, the growing trend is for college career/ placement centers to charge either a participation fee or to suggest a donation.

To garner a wider range of applicants of varying ages and experiences, consider commercially sponsored job events, which offer a multitude of advantages over college and community events. The sponsors promote the events widely throughout the print and broadcast media, on the Web, and often through direct mailings. They have the graphic artists, the copywriters, the public relations specialists, and other resources who work together to promote the event effectively and professionally. These well-organized events draw large crowds of job seekers. The overall cost of participation in these events, however, is significantly higher than for college or community events. A booth rental fee can run anywhere from $200 to more than $1,500, and there may be carpet rental fees and drayage fees as well. You will also pay for ad space if you want to run a display ad in the event guide. If you're considering this method, be sure to read Chapter 8 thoroughly.

In some communities, job fairs are organized as a community service by local businesses such as the local newspaper or radio stations. Other local organizations or agencies, such as the Chamber of Commerce or Private Industry Council, may put together job fairs in partnership with other community businesses or agencies. The cost of participation in these fairs will vary, but they are generally less expensive than the commercially produced events.

Don't overlook local community fairs and festivals as potential recruitment opportunities. If the library is planning to have a table or booth at the Tomato Festival, Family Day in the Park, or Christmas Fair, make sure staff participating in these events know about current vacancies and have job announcements and application forms to distribute at the booth.

ATTEND CONFERENCES

Conferences like the annual American Library Association Conference offer job centers and the opportunity for on-site interviewing. Associations of computer and technical professionals and a host of other professional associations also offer similar services.

Some association and trade-show conferences also allow employers to rent booth space for the purpose of recruitment. I participated in an excellent opportunity for staff recruitment several years ago. At the annual conference of the California Association for Bilingual Education, held in San Jose in 1996, the association combined the trade show with their career-placement center. Both trade exhibitors and employers were intermixed on the exhibit floor, giving employers higher visibility at the event and the chance to promote job openings to individuals who might not have necessarily been thinking about a new job. For the conference registrants who might have been uncomfortable visiting a separate placement center for fear their current employer would find out, this setup provided an easy means of gaining access to potential employers.

Downsides of this method do of course exist. They can include the overall cost, and the fact that most associations hold only one conference a year. Whether these are indeed downsides, however, depends upon how effective they prove to be in your recruitment efforts.

ENCOURAGE EMPLOYEE REFERRALS

A low-cost method of recruitment is an employee-referral program. These are in-house incentive programs that award a monetary or other bonus to employees who refer an applicant who is subsequently hired by the library. The underlying theory of these programs is that employees associate with other people in the profession or same line of work and will only refer applicants who would be a credit to them.

This method is most effective when it is an established, formal program. The program should include regular communication with staff about job vacancies, ongoing staffing needs, and the minimum qualifications required of the positions. Staff should have a thorough understanding of how the referral program works.

CONSIDER EMPLOYMENT AGENCIES AND SERVICES

Employment agencies specialize in providing employers with qualified applicants. They solicit and prescreen applicants for the employer—at a cost. Either the employer or applicant—or in some cases both—is charged a fee. If you are considering this method, carefully consider its cost effectiveness as opposed to if the services were performed in-house. Since all agencies do not provide the same quality of service, take the time to seek referrals and references before selecting one.

A less expensive alternative to employment agencies are publicly funded services. These are usually state and federally funded agencies whose goal is to decrease the unemployment rate in the area. They will try to match applicants with employers. The exact services will vary from one agency to another.

If you plan to select a private employment agency, try to find one that is either familiar with or has experience filling library positions. Make sure the agency clearly understands the position, and the characteristics, skills, and experiences required of the applicants. There are today a number of firms that specialize in library placements. Appendix A lists several of these firms.

INVESTIGATE EXECUTIVE RECRUITERS AND SEARCH FIRMS

Executive recruiters and search firms differ from employment agencies not only in their focus but also in the mode in which they operate. In general, employment agencies acquire potential applicants through advertisements, so their pool is comprised of individuals who are seeking positions. Executive recruiters and search firms familiarize themselves with the vacancy and then often survey the field of individuals holding similar positions to identify those who are a potential match for the vacancy. They then contact these individuals to entice them to apply for the vacant position.

For organizations that lack sufficient personnel staff to conduct a quality search recruitment effort, or for those who prefer to utilize outside assistance, executive search firms can provide varying levels of assistance. That level depends upon your preferences and the services provided by the firm. The following services are typical of those commonly provided:

- *development of job descriptions and announcements.* Working with appropriate library staff, the firm will write a job description and job announcement for the vacant position.

A Legal Issue to Be Aware of

If you opt to contract with an executive search firm, employment agency, or any outside source, that individual or firm becomes your agent. You need to familiarize yourself with the law of agency, based upon the Latin "qui facit per alium, facit per se"—which translates into "he who acts through another is deemed in law to do it himself."

- *identify potential applicants.* The firm will use a variety of means ranging from advertising to "head hunting" to recruit applicants.
- *applicant screening.* The firm will review and assess all job applications and applicants. Depending on your preference, they will forward the applications of all individuals meeting the job requirements, or only of the most competitive three or five applications.
- *interview scheduling and interviewing.* The firm will schedule interviews and, if you wish, also participate in the interviews.
- *reference and background checks.* The firm will perform reference checks and background checks on the applicants' work history, education, and retail criteria.
- *job-offer negotiations.* The firm can help you negotiate salary and other benefits with potential new employees.

LOOK INTO INTERNAL RECRUITMENT

Some employers prefer to promote from within. Internal recruitment has a number of advantages, ranging from boosting overall employee morale by demonstrating a career ladder within the organization, to having an applicant pool that is already familiar with the library, its operations, and clientele. The potential disadvantages are also many, ranging from a possibly very limited applicant pool, to creating awkward situations if an external applicant is hired over a qualified existing staff member who may have expected to fill the position.

WHICH METHOD IS BEST?

There's no one recruitment method that works best for every job vacancy and every library. A method's effectiveness varies depending upon factors including the type and level of position for which you are recruiting, the labor pool in your geographic area and in general for the type of position, other competitors in the area, your skill at recruiting, and what financial resources you have (see Figure 6–1). Determining the best way to recruit for your library can only be done after you've tried different methods and have gathered and analyzed data on the quantity and quality of the applicants yielded by each. Figure 6–2 gives an overview of the level of resources necessary for different strategies.

Although the overall success of each method we've discussed does not appear to have been studied specifically in the recruitment of library staff, various studies have been done within the business world.

Figure 6–1 Identifying External Costs

This list is designed to help you identify potential external costs of utilizing the specific recruitment methods. You also need to carefully consider the staff resources you will need to devote to the specific methods chosen.

ADVERTISING

Classified Advertising
Number of lines in classified ad × cost per line × number of times the ad is run = $_____

Display Advertising
Graphic artist/design cost + camera-ready copy cost + (cost of ad space
+ number of times the ad is run) = $_____

Internet Advertising
You need to contact the host of the Web site or administrator of the listserv on which
you wish to advertise your opening to determine appropriateness and fees.

Radio Advertising
Amount of time (measured in seconds) × number of times the ad is aired × air-time cost
(which varies depending upon the time of the day the ad is aired, as well as the day) = $_____

Television Advertising
Ad production costs + air-time costs (varies with the time the ad is aired,
station/channel used, etc.) + number of times aired = $_____

ON-CAMPUS RECRUITING

Service Fee
The college or school may charge the employer a fee for use of their services.

On-site Interviewing
The college or school may charge a fee for use of interview facilities.

Job/Career Fairs and Events
Participation fee: charged by many colleges, this fee is often waived for employers representing public and government agencies or nonprofit organizations.

Display rental fee: applicable only if you intend to rent a display. If so, you may also need to invest some resources into developing artwork to be used, if you have not already done so.

(Continued)

Figure 6–1 Continued

COMMERCIALLY PRODUCED JOB FAIRS AND EVENTS
Exhibit Space Rental Fee: varies depending upon whether you want a full booth space or smaller booth or table space. A full booth usually accommodates an 8' × 10' display. The smaller booth usually can accommodate either a tabletop or 6' × 8' display.

Carpeting fee: carpeting in the booth space is often only provided for a fee.

Drayage fee: if you ship your display to the event, a drayage fee is usually charged to get it to your exhibit spot.

Display rental fee: applicable if you need to rent a display. If so, you may also need to invest some resources into developing artwork to be used on the display.

Printing fee: applicable if you utilize an external printer to produce the recruitment materials you distribute.

CONFERENCES
Participation fee: may be referred to as an employer fee.

Exhibit fee: if renting exhibit space, the fees similar to those for commercially produced job fairs and events also may apply.

EMPLOYMENT AGENCIES AND SERVICES, AND EXECUTIVE RECRUITERS AND SEARCH FIRMS
The costs associated with these methods vary widely. You need to contact specific agencies and firms regarding their services and fees.

David Terpstra of the University of Mississippi's School of Business Administration conducted a survey of 201 human-resources executives "to discover which recruiting and selection methods produce the best employees for their organizations (all had 200-plus employees)."[1] The results of his survey show that the top three recruitment sources were employee referrals, college recruiting, and executive search firms. The other six sources that appeared on the survey were professional associations, want ads, direct applications, private employment agencies, public employment agencies, and unions. Interestingly, the most widespread method of recruitment, want ads, was rated fifth in producing the best employees.

According to Terpestra, the three top sources "all seem more likely to yield the types of motivated, multiskilled workers required for success in our new environment." "These sources are thought to tap different labor-market segments and applicant populations, and thus may lead to better educated, more motivated and, with the exception of college recruiting, more experienced candidates (p. 16)." Since the study

---

Figure 6–2 Recruitment Resource Levels

RECRUITMENT ACTIVITIES EVERY LIBRARY CAN UNDERTAKE (REQUIRING MINIMAL FINANCIAL AND STAFFING RESOURCES)

Set up an internal recruitment program

Establish an informal employee-referral program (offering no financial incentives)

Advertise (classified)

Participate in local, on-campus recruiting at high schools and colleges

Take part in community-sponsored job and career events

RECRUITMENT ACTIVITIES REQUIRING SOME LEVEL OF STAFFING AND FINANCIAL RESOURCES

Participate in commercially produced job events

Participate in nonlocal college career events

Place classified ads in national publications or display ads in regional publications

Use employment agencies

Establish a formal employee-referral program (offering financial and other incentives)

RECRUITMENT ACTIVITIES REQUIRING A SIGNIFICANT INVESTMENT OF FINANCIAL AND/OR STAFFING RESOURCES

Recruit at conferences

Place of display ad in national publications

Use executive recruiters and search firms

---

cited no information about the types of industries represented by the executives surveyed, or the nature of the positions, it's impossible to determine whether these findings are relevant for library recruitment. However, it does offer food for thought, since time and again we hear the comment that "libraries need to be run more like businesses."

NOTE

1. See David E. Terpstra. "The Search for Effective Methods." *HR Focus* (May 1996): 16–17.

7 RECRUITMENT ADVERTISING

The movie *Field of Dreams* immortalized the phrase, "If you build it, they will come." In reality, the best and brightest applicants will not flock to your library simply because it exists. You have to bring these individuals to your doors by recruitment advertising—an integral mainstay of every recruitment program.

The scope of recruitment advertising can range from the simple placement of a help-wanted advertisement in the local newspaper to the development of a multifaceted, multimedia campaign. The extent of your efforts will depend primarily upon the overall number of vacancies expected in the near future, and on the financial and staff resources available to you. But regardless of the extent of the campaign to be undertaken, every library should have a recruitment advertising "package" ready on the shelf (see page 64 for a worksheet to get you started). The package should include items such as some standard copy about the benefits offered, positive aspects of the library as an employer, and supporting graphics. These are all pieces that, if they haven't already been developed, should be. They are inexpensive to produce and a necessary component of any recruitment effort. They are the basics upon which you can build your recruitment advertising.

ASK YOURSELF FOUR CRUCIAL QUESTIONS

Before embarking upon developing a recruitment advertising "package" or program, a number of factors need to be considered to help you develop the direction and scope of your campaign. Answering the following questions will help you begin to mold your new ad package.

1. *What is the immediate goal of your recruitment advertising?* Are you trying to solicit as many job applicants as possible for vacant or expected vacancies? Or are you trying to attract just a select number of highly qualified applicants for your available openings? For vacancies in general classifications, such as library pages, or basic clerical positions, your goal may be to get the highest number of applicants from which you can select applicants. For specialized or technical positions, you may want only a few, very highly qualified applicants.

Worksheet: Developing Your Recruitment Advertising

OVERALL GUIDEPOSTS

- What is the immediate goal of your recruitment advertising?
- How many, and what, vacancies do you anticipate advertising for in the upcoming year?
- What resources are available to you for recruitment advertising?
- What is your time frame for developing your recruitment advertising?

FOR ADVERTISEMENT OF SPECIFIC POSITIONS/CLASSIFICATIONS

- Who is your target audience?
- What medium(s) will be utilized?
    - —Newspapers
    - —Professional journals
    - —Job lines
    - —Internet
    - —Radio
    - —Direct Mail

FOR THE JOB ADVERTISEMENT YOU DEVELOPED

- Does it have a hook that grabs the reader's attention or interest?
- Does the body of the ad "sell" the positive aspects of the position or the library as an employer?
- Does the body provide a brief description of the position and either the minimum or desired qualifications?
- Does the ad end with a call to action for those ready to apply?
- Does the ad contain sufficient contact information and/or information on how to apply for the position?
- Is the ad in compliance with existing advertising laws?
- Have you developed an evaluation process to determine the effectiveness of the ad and the medium(s) selected?

2. *How many and what type of vacancies do you expect to recruit for in the upcoming year, or next two to three years?* Get as accurate an estimate as possible as to the number and nature of expected vacancies in the next year. You will need this information to help you determine whether you should develop several targeted ads, or a single ad template that can be easily adapted and re-used with varying text. Review these expected vacancies with an eye to whether special skills or education are needed, and whether you have only a limited pool of individuals to draw from on a state or national level.

3. *What monetary and staff resources can be allocated to recruitment advertising?* In the real world, we're unfortunately often confined to working within the resources available to us, especially in relation to financial resources. However, you may have some flexibility in the staff assistance available to you, depending upon your local situation. If a graphic artist is employed in the larger entity of which the library is a part, or if technical staff exist within the multimedia production department of your overall entity (such as corporation, college, county), you may be able to utilize their services as needed on a no- or low-cost, fee-recovery basis.

4. *What, if any, time constraints exist for development of your recruitment advertising package or program?* The amount that can reasonably be accomplished is often determined by the amount of time available for development. You must devote adequate time to developing effective recruitment advertising. The adverse effects of a poor or inappropriate advertising program can do irreparable damage not only to your recruitment efforts but also to your institution or company.

Bearing your answers to these questions in mind, let's review the six steps and considerations involved in developing a recruitment advertisement.

FIVE STEPS TO DEVELOPING A RECRUITMENT ADVERTISEMENT

STEP 1. TARGET YOUR AUDIENCE

Before developing an ad, you need to know exactly who your target is. Effective advertisements elicit and/or speak to the interests or concerns of the targeted candidates. If your resources or situation permit development of only a single ad in which the job text will be substituted as needed, the ad template still needs to address your target group, so know to whom you are "talking."

In Chapter 4, you focused on determining the desired characteristics, skills, and abilities of the individuals you hope to recruit to your library. These are the individuals your ad should target. Remember that your recruitment ads are a communication mechanism between your library and the potential applicant.

STEP 2. SELECT THE MEDIUM

Pay careful attention to selecting the most appropriate medium(s) for reaching your targeted audience. Which medium is utilized the most by the targeted audience? The most commonly used mediums for professional positions are the newspaper and professional journals or job lines, with local radio stations often used for recruitment of support positions. And the Internet is becoming a common resource. Magazines and television are seldom used, primarily due to cost. In selecting the medium for your job advertising, consider which will be most effective and economical in reaching your targeted audience. Let's take a look at the various mediums.

Newspapers

As mentioned earlier, local newspaper job advertising remains one of the most commonly used mediums in job recruitment. Help-wanted ads and display ads placed in local newspapers are effective in reaching potential applicants within the community or nearby geographic regions. They are fairly inexpensive and easy to create and run in the local newspapers. Because of the daily publication of most newspapers, job vacancies can be quickly posted.

Professional Journals

Very effective at reaching large, targeted audiences, job ads run in professional journals are more expensive than those in local newspapers. However, for professional vacancies, placement of job notices in professional library journals is highly recommended. Since professional journals tend to be published only monthly, make sure the time line for solicitation of job applications fits comfortably within the journal publisher's deadline for placement of the ad, and the printing and distribution schedule for that specific issue of the journal. Appendix B lists some periodicals in which jobs can be advertised.

Job Lines

Many libraries, universities, counties, cities, and corporations operate job lines, but their effectiveness and reach are limited only to those individuals with a great enough interest in working for the organization that they are willing to call the specific job line on a regular basis. National or association-run job lines are more effective in recruiting a wider base of applicants. A number of statewide library associations, like the California Library Association, and professional library associations, such as the Special Libraries Association, operate job lines and usually charge only a nominal fee to place vacancies on them. Appendix C contains a list of these and other job lines.

Internet

Given the widespread use of the Internet, it's value in disseminating information about job openings is without question. The big question, however, is whether the Internet is effective in reaching the desired applicants.

If your library has a Web page, think about posting your openings there. This is a low- or no-cost means of providing job vacancy information. Individuals interested in working for your library may check your Web site for job information. Be aware that if this is your only advertising focus, then your applicant base will be very limited. Plus, those individuals visiting your Web page may or may not be doing it for employment purposes.

A variety of commercial and professional association Web sites are widely known for posting library job openings, and these can be good places to advertise professional positions. General job sites can also be useful for getting out the word on lower-level openings. The advantage of having your vacancies posted on these sites is that they're frequently consulted by library job seekers. The cost for posting on these sites ranges from no charge to a significant expense.

A low or no-cost method of distributing job announcements over the Internet is by posting them on relevant listservs. Listservs abound. And job announcements posted there can reach literally thousands of people in a matter of minutes. But be aware that not all listservs allow the posting of job announcements, and those that do usually permit only listserv subscribers to do so. You should check with the listserv administrator regarding their policy. There's no charge for subscription unless the listserv is restricted.

Appendix D selectively highlights a variety of library-related listservs, as well as subscription information. If desired, you can subscribe to a listserv, post your notice, then unsubscribe from the list. But if you decide to remain subscribed for a while, you'll have the opportunity to study the types, frequency, and job announcements of your competition. Appendices E and F offer Web sites where jobs are listed.

Radio

If you want to draw a lot of applicants from the community, advertising on the local radio station is one option. The advantage of this medium is it raises the visibility of the library's services, and of the library as an employer in the community. The potential downside is that you may receive a huge number of applications from individuals without appropriate qualifications. Since radio announcements of vacant positions or calls for applicants are generally limited to less than thirty seconds, only brief information about vacancies can be announced. Radio ads have a very short "shelf life" in comparison to some other media.

Local Television

The advantages and disadvantages of advertising job openings on local television are similar to those of radio. Television advertising, if done properly, allows you to graphically showcase the library. However, the production costs can be significant unless you have access to production facilities within your library, college or organization.

Direct Mail

Most professional and trade associations and organizations give you the option of purchasing either their entire mailing list, or obtaining subsets of their lists by geographic area or other breakdowns, such as specialty. The advantage of direct mail is that it often reaches the best and brightest individuals who may not be currently thinking about a job change but who might consider a change. These are individuals you might not reach via advertisements on job lines, or in the job section of newspapers or professional journals because they are not actively looking. Other than the cost—depending on how large the mailing is—there are no major drawbacks to this method.

Which Medium?

As you consider which medium (or mediums) will be the most cost effective for reaching your recruitment goals, remember to examine them in relation to the geography and demographics of the individuals you hope to reach. Do you have an adequate applicant pool locally, or do you have to recruit from a wide geographic area? Several media have far-reaching geographic coverage, but within these you need to look at the specific channels under consideration for their effectiveness. For example, if you choose newspaper advertising/ classifieds as your primary tool, for any newspaper under consideration, find out the geographical statistics on the distribution of the paper in terms of both of newstands and subscribers. Also determine and consider the newspaper's frequency, its readership, and if there is an Internet version of the paper.

The importance of knowing the demographics of the individuals you seek to recruit is important when determining the best medium to reach them. For example, if you are seeking bilingual, Spanish-speaking staff, advertising your positions in bilingual or Spanish-language newspapers or radio stations might be appropriate. Or if you are recruiting high-level, technical visionaries to head your library automation unit, you may want to consider advertising on selected Internet Web sites or listservs, or in frequently published industry news publications. Determining the medium and its specific advertising venue(s) requires taking the time to research their specific advantages and disadvantages, as well as the individuals they reach.

STEP 3. DEVELOP THE JOB ADVERTISEMENT

Text

Hopefully, your resources do not restrict you to a three- or four-line classified ad. In three or four classified lines you are basically running a job "announcement," not an advertisement. A job advertisement, which may consist of just text, allows you to promote one or more job openings through three basic components: the hook, the body, and the closing call to action.

Your advertisement starts with a "hook"—a means of grabbing the reader's interest. The hook is by far the most difficult component of the ad. Your hook needs to grab the interest not only of the reader but also of the specific, "right" people you want to recruit. The hook needs to immediately appeal to them and make them want to continue reading the ad. This is where really knowing the target of your recruitment activities pays off.

Your hook can take a variety of approaches. It can stress the benefits of the position, both monetary and nonmonetary, or of working for the specific employer. A high-paying salary or not-too-common benefits such as telecommuting or flexible schedules can attract the attention of certain individuals. If there are no exceptional monetary or job-related benefits, you can stress circumstantial ones. Some individuals are more interested in working in a place with fun, sun, and sand, or where there is a good quality of life, rather than in a position's salary and benefits. Or your hook can appeal to the applicant's sense of responsibility to the community or the common good (especially if there are insignificant monetary or other benefits of the position). For instance, the successful applicant will be able to effect positive changes in the lives of children, new immigrants, or the like. Your hook can also throw down a challenge: you could be seeking a fearless individual to shake up the organization by reorganizing and improving the management structure of the library.

An advertisement that starts with "the library has an opening for (job title)" followed by a summary of the job duties doesn't inspire a person to read on. Effective hooks don't simply provide information, they speak to the reader. For example, the hook of an ad recently run to recruit a director of a public library in Wisconsin read, "If you are a person interested in community and breaking new ground in library management, consider joining us in a challenging journey blending traditional library services with new opportunities created by emerging technologies." This hook speaks to the reader, piques interest, and entices further investigation.

If your plans include direct mail to distribute your recruitment advertisement or job announcement, you then have the flexibility to include your hook in a cover letter instead of the actual job ad text, if desired. However, you should take advantage of having two opportunities to grab the reader's attention both in the cover letter and in the text of the advertisement. To give you an idea of an effective letter "hook," take a look at the first paragraph of the cover letter sent with a job announcement for a position in Hialeah, Florida, which appeared as Figure 2–2.

Once you've got your hook, it's time to move on to the body of the text. This should contain sufficient information about the position and desired experience, skills, and characteristics to help readers determine if they are a possible match for the job. But the body of the ad needs to contain more than just a brief job description and minimum qualifications. The body is where you have the opportunity to promote the benefits of the position and to excite the reader about the potential of working for your library or the greater organization. This is where you sell your position to the potential candidates, to illuminate the best features and services of your library. This is also where professionals look for information about the library and its parent organization or company. The positive aspects of the potential employer are often just as important to professionals as the positive aspects of the vacant position.

Remember that your ad should include not just the demands and responsibilities of the job but also the rewards. It should be noted that some employers list the downsides of the position as a way of screening out applicants unwilling to work under certain conditions. This tactic could have a very negative effect upon the image of your library, however, so this is not recommended. There are many more effective methods of screening that don't give your library a bad name.

In developing the body of your advertisement, remember to provide enough information that readers can determine their interest in and suitability for the position. Keep the text concise, and easy to read. It keeps the reader moving forward to the end of the ad.

The closure of the ad should motivate qualified individuals to apply for the position. Supply either information on how to apply or a person to contact for further information. Make it as easy as possible for the applicant to secure either additional information about the position or any necessary application forms. If your library has a Web site, make the full job description and application forms available there. Be willing to fax full job descriptions or forms upon request. Remember that each potential applicant could someday be your boss or the library director.

Also be sure to keep all staff informed of your recruitment efforts and planned advertisements. Your staff can function as an informal medium of advertisement through both the patrons they come in contact with and their own personal connections. They can be powerful allies or enemies in your recruitment efforts, so keep them apprised of the benefits of recruiting new staff so that they do not feel threatened by the process. Provide them with advance copies of the ads so that they will be informed and armed with current and correct information.

After you've developed and run one or more advertisements, build in time to evaluate your efforts. How effective was the medium used? Did the advertisement work well? You can build in a special code for the specific medium used in each ad and ask applicants to refer to that code when requesting information or submitting an application. Or you can include a survey on your application forms—or on a separate form—asking how the applicant heard of the position and what was enticing. You can also do a more thorough survey of new employees. Once you have gathered the data, analyze them. Also take the time to evaluate the quality of the applicants you drew in via a particular medium or specific ad. And most important, use the evaluation to refine your recruitment efforts as needed. A good recruitment advertising campaign will only have a shelf life of three to four years before it begins to lose its effectiveness.

STEP 4. KNOW THE RELEVANT LEGAL ISSUES

If you're not familiar with state and federal laws regarding advertising, make sure you take the time to review them. You may already be familiar with many, such as those against intentionally advertising for job vacancies that do not exist, or running ads that refer to race or sex. But the legal landscape is constantly changing. If you are in doubt about any part of your advertising, be sure to seek legal counsel.

Be sure to familiarize yourself with these and other relevant advertising laws.

- Age Discrimination in Employment Act (U.S. Code Title 29)
  The following appears in Section 623e:
  It shall be unlawful for an employer, labor organization, or employment agency to print or publish, or cause to be printed or published, any notice or advertisement relating to employment by such an employer or membership in or any classification or referral for employment by such a labor organization, or relating to any classification or referral of employment by such an employment agency, indicating any preference, limitation, specification, or discrimination, based on age.

  The prohibitions in this chapter shall be limited to individuals who are at least 40 years of age.

- Americans with Disabilities Act (U.S. Code Title 42, Chapter 126)
  The following appears in Section 12115:
  Every employer, employment agency, labor union, or joint labor-management committee covered under this subchapter shall post notices in an accessible format to applicants, employees, and members describing the applicable provision of this chapter, in the manner prescribed by section 2000e-10 of this title.

- Civil Rights Act (U.S. Code Title 42)
  The following appears in Section 2000e-3(b):
  It shall be unlawful employment practice for an employer, labor organization, employment agency or joint labor-management committee controlling apprenticeship or other training or retraining, including on the job training programs, to print or publish, or cause to be printed or published, any notice or advertisement relating to employment such an employer or membership in any classification or referral for employment by such a labor organization, or relating to any classification or referral of employment by such an employment agency, or relating to admission to, or employment in, any program established to provide apprenticeship or other training by such a joint labor-management committee, indicating any preference, limitation, specification, or discrimination, based upon religion, sex, or national origin

except that such a notice or advertisement may indicate a preference, limitation, specification, or discrimination based on religion, sex, or national origin when religion, sex, or national origin is a bona fide occupational qualification for employment.

STEP 5. MAINTAIN AN ADVERTISING PACKAGE

Earlier in this chapter we discussed the need to maintain a "recruitment package" that is ready to use as needed. An effective package enables you to easily implement a variety of recruitment activities and provides you with all the information you need to be competitive. An effective package is always current and is as essential as your wallet or billfold. Like your wallet, it contains everything you might need to get by on a daily basis.

Although every library's recruitment package will differ, there are some core materials that should be included:

- camera-ready advertising templates (for classified and/or display advertisements)
- camera-ready copy of the library logo, symbol, or letterhead
- basic library information, such as hours, services, collections, branches
- library organization chart
- if applicable, organization chart showing where the library falls within the corporation
- information on job benefits offered to all employees (such as medical, retirement)
- information on the community (if a public library), on the college/university (if an academic library), or on the company or organization (if a special library)
- information on the general geographic area, such as cost of living, demographics, transportation

Remember that the materials in the recruitment "package" are there for one reason only: to help you in your recruitment efforts. They are sales tools and should reflect information in a positive rather than a negative manner.

3 MAXIMIZING YOUR PARTICIPATION IN JOB EVENTS

Your recruitment plans are likely to include participation in job fairs and events. Whether your plans call for distributing job information at the summer job fair at the local high school or staffing a booth at a national professional conference, a variety of activities and recruitment tools can help you maximize your participation and effectiveness at these events. Let's start with the tools.

Before you participate in job fairs, conferences, or community fairs, you need to devote some time and resources to development of a recruitment display, or to review and update of an existing display or, at minimum, table banner. These events draw a large number of participants, so be prepared to make a good impression. You want the participants at these events to perceive your library as a good potential employer. The image you project should be professional and should reinforce the one you determined in Chapter 5.

Start your development activities with a few field trips. If you can, visit the specific job fairs, conferences, and other events in which you may be interested in participating. Once you arrive at the event, be prepared to give yourself sufficient time to make at least two "walk-throughs" of the event floor. Note the job seekers the event draws. At first glance, do these job seekers appear to be an appropriate pool for your recruitment needs (for example, primarily professional, or blue-collar workers)? Is the event drawing a sufficient number of job seekers to meet your needs?

Take note of the physical environment and facilities in which the events are held. Note the space provided to employers. Does the facility have a low or high ceiling? Does an electrical outlet appear available in each of the booths?

Next, focus your attention on the employers. In general, what types of employers are participating? What do you perceive the percentage of employers from government or the public sector, corporations, private or small-businesses, or the education sector to be? Is the event drawing Fortune 500 employers? What proportion of the employers are potential competitors for the sample applicants you seek to recruit? Be sure to jot down your impressions for later use and review.

Now study the employers' displays. Examine how successful each one is at promoting an image and attracting applicants to their booth. Do the employer and the display appear professional? And if not, why?

What message is the employer conveying? Which displays impressed you and why?

Beyond the physical display, pay attention to the staff in the booth. Is their manner, conversation, and interaction with potential applicants an asset or a detriment? And why? Do they significantly add or detract from the image being promoted by the employer, and why?

Use this opportunity to pick up the various materials distributed by the employers. Take note of which seem to be of most interest to the job seekers. Study and select the best materials as examples you can refer to for developing your own materials. Learn whatever you can about how the employers are effectively reaching the applicants they seek through this recruitment method. Because college career events and commercially sponsored events draw different audiences, notice any differences in the ways the employers effectively draw applicants to their booth. Pay special attention to the display, staffing, and materials distributed by employers who are potential competitors for the applicants you hope to seek. Page 77 is a worksheet to help you record your observations.

Now that you've gained an understanding of the environment in which you'll be participating, it's time to think about your display needs. There are only a few basic types of displays that form the foundation for a variety of configurations.

Worksheet: Event Preparticipation

Event Name:

Sponsor:

Location:

Date:

Impression of event attendance: ___ High ___ Average ___ Low

FACILITY ARRANGEMENTS
Does the facility have a high or low ceiling?

What is the lighting like?

How much space is provided to each employer?

Does there appear to be access to electrical outlets in some or all of the booths?

TYPES OF JOB SEEKERS IN ATTENDANCE

Professional? Blue Collar?

New to work force?

TYPES OF EMPLOYERS IN ATTENDANCE

Percentage of employers from the following sectors

Corporate

Private or small business

Public sector

Educational sector

List employers that are potential competitors
(Pick up copies of their literature.)

Which employers are drawing large numbers of potential applicants to their booths, and why?

What types of literature are they distributing?

Do their displays convey a specific message, and if so, what?

Are the individuals staffing their booths a significantly valuable asset, and why?

CONSIDER A VARIETY OF DISPLAYS

POP-UP DISPLAYS

Gone are the days when a crew of skilled workmen was required to assemble a display. Engineering advances make today's displays, called "pop-ups," lighter and simpler to assemble. Constructed of either aluminum or some other light-weight metal or polymer, the display frames can be packed and shipped in a very small container and literally "popped up" in less than a minute. These displays are available in a curved or arced frame, or in a straight or flat frame. Panels are then easily attached to the frame or support braces via magnetized strips. The panels can take many formats ranging from fabric, upon which artwork can be attached, to photomural panels. Lights, shelves, and display boxes can easily be added to the display. These pop-up displays are available in standard sizes such as 6' × 8', 8' × 10', 10' × 10', and larger, as well as in table-top display sizes.

The transport cases for these displays have also been updated. Both upright and horizontal transport cases with wheels and handles are available. These roll cases are even designed so that they can be strapped or snapped together for easy toting.

The biggest advantage of pop-up displays is their ease of transport and set up. On many occasions I've transported an 8' × 10' display that, with photomural panels, into two upright wheeled cases. By myself, I'm able to set up the full display in less than fifteen minutes.

MODULAR DISPLAYS

Modular displays come in many shapes, sizes, and styles of construction. Some consist of hinged panels, whereas others utilize a variety of interlocking curved- and straight-back frames. The advantage of modular displays is they provide flexibility in overall exhibit design. You can construct any exhibit configuration, and can easily move from a 10' display to one several times that size simply by adding on other modules or components.

However, there are potential disadvantages to modular displays. They may require skilled workmen to assemble and disassemble them. They may be more costly to transport. And the services of a drayage contractor may be necessary.

If you plan to participate in conference or trade shows, or commercially produced job fairs, you will undoubtedly utilize the services of a drayage company or contractor because of the potential size and shipping requirements of the modular display. Drayage companies or contractors are responsible for exhibit materials at trade shows, and other events and perform a number of services, including receipt and transportation of your display and other materials to your specific exhibit space at the event site. They remove and store your display transport cases during the event, and return them to your booth space at the end of the event. They also move your transport-ready display to the loading/shipping area of the event site for carrier pickup.

TABLE-TOP DISPLAYS

Table-top displays come in a variety of formats, ranging from pop-up to three-panel, hinged displays. Because they are smaller, they are easier to transport than full-standing displays. They are also less expensive to purchase and transport.

DETERMINE YOUR DISPLAY NEEDS

The best way to get a good, working knowledge of the different types and features of exhibits is, if geographically possible, to visit a display showroom. Display suppliers and manufacturers are usually more than happy to show you their products. Or, if there is no showroom in your area, determine the type of the display you may want and ask the supplier to send a salesperson to your site with a sample display. Some of the vendors listed in Appendix G have Web sites. But before you get to that point, let's look at some basic factors that need to be considered.

PHYSICAL ENVIRONMENT

After you have visited the events in which you are interested in participating, you'll have a good sense of the general physical environment in which the display will be used. Will you need primarily a display that fits within a very small booth space, or should you get a display that makes an impression in a very large space? Or do most of the events provide only table space? Do the facilities have a low ceiling, limiting the height of the actual display or attachments such as overhead lights? Select a display size that will give you maximum use. If the size of the area in which you'll be exhibiting varies only slightly, you many want to consider a hinged panel display that can accommodate these size differences.

Another consideration is whether the display will be used indoors, outdoors, or both. Some displays and fabrics are better suited for outdoor use than indoor use; outdoor displays need to withstand the elements.

EASE OF ASSEMBLY AND TEAR DOWN

Pop-up displays offer easy assembly and dismantling. Modular displays also offer easy assembly, but some may also require skilled laborers to assemble them. In selecting a display, consider whether you need a display that can be easily set up by one or two people, or if hiring workers is an option. If easy assembly is a requirement—especially if a wide range of staff may be called upon to participate in the event—don't take the sales representative's word as to the ease of set up and tear down of a specific display. Ask to try it yourself. You'd be surprised at how many squashed fingers and bruised toes you could subject yourself to in setting up a so-called easy-to-assemble display.

PORTABILITY AND TRANSPORTABILITY

Will most of the events you plan to participate in be within reasonable driving distance, or will they be geographically dispersed over a wide area? Will you or your staff most likely be transporting the display, or do you intend regularly to ship the display to its destination? If you plan to transport the display personally, the size and ease of transportability of the display will be a significant consideration in your product selection. If the display requires a forklift for set up or shipping, you will be paying a high fee for drayage services.

   Durability is a consideration unless you have an unlimited budget. The display frames can be adapted to a variety of exhibit purposes. Only the artwork needs to be updated. Unfortunately, ease of transportability does not necessarily correlate to durability.

STORAGE

Before selecting a display product, find out if you have space in-house or at another facility to store the display. If you do, get precise information as to the size of the storage area. Your stored display will need to fit into this space unless you have the resources to contract for off-site storage and drayage services.

EVALUATE PURCHASING VERSUS RENTING

You have the option of either purchasing a display or renting it. Your decision to purchase may depend on a number of factors other than just cost effectiveness—factors such as the proximity of the nearest facility where you can rent a display, and other potential uses of the display. Even if you purchase a full-standing display with photomural panels, you can also purchase blank panels that can be used with the

Worksheet: Display and Event Cost-Estimate Form

DISPLAY COSTS

Display purchase cost (one-time cost): _____

Display rental cost: _____

Display graphic design and art-work costs (one-time cost): _____

Display rental accessory costs (such as counters, shelving, lights): _____

EVENT-ASSOCIATED COSTS

Participation or booth rental fee: _____

Display and materials shipping and insurance fee, if applicable: _____

Drayage fees, if applicable: _____

Labor charges to assemble and dismantle display, if applicable: _____

Booth carpeting fee, if applicable: _____

Booth cleaning fee, if desired: _____

Additional chairs or tables in the booth, if desired: _____

Electrical fees (if needed): _____

Telephone fees (if needed): _____

Audio-visual or computer equipment rental fee: _____

Special advertising fee in the event guide or literature: _____

Printing of materials distributed at the event: _____

Total: _____

frame. In addition to recruitment events, consider how else the display can be used in library events. For instance, could it help promote thematic library promotions or celebrations? Or do your children's librarians have a sporadic need to display the work of essay or artwork contestants? A worksheet to help you in estimating costs is on page 81.

Most employers purchase a new display. Used displays are available, but their cost and condition vary, and it's more difficult to find suppliers of used displays. You need to carefully consider whether a new, used, or rented display best meets your needs.

Some rental services are willing to "customize" their displays for you. For instance, you're not limited to renting a "package" display and can request a mix of panel colors and fabrics. Many services will also try to configure display modules to meet your specifications.

If you decide to rent a display, make sure you know what you're getting yourself into. Make sure you read the rental agreement and note what your liability is if the display is damaged, lost in shipment, or stolen. Make sure you understand exactly what the rental fee covers. For instance, does it include delivery?

SIX WAYS TO MAKE THE MOST OF JOB FAIRS

1. DISPLAY GRAPHICS AND ART WORK

Up to this point we've discussed the display hardware, but we have yet to address the display graphics. If you have decided to invest the time and resources into taking part in job events, devote the necessary resources to secure professional graphic design services or, if you have a graphics person on staff, at least consult a professional. Remember your display impacts how prospective applicants perceive your library as a viable employer, and promotes your library's image or message. Your graphics need to tell potential applicants who you are, what you are (a library? a bank?), and the benefits of, or some reasons why, they should want to work for your library. The graphics need to grab a person's attention. Your graphics should be designed by a professional.

2. USE BANNERS AND TABLE DRAPES

If the primary job events you'll be participating in are local community fairs, or college and high school job fairs, your needs may not warrant a display but simply a banner or table drape with the library or organization's name may be on it. However, it is imperative that potential applicants know what employer you represent. Depending upon your image in the community, potential applicants may be specifically seeking you out, so make it easy for them.

Banners and table drapes are available in various shapes, sizes, and fabrics. Banners can be ordered that attach (velcro works great!) to just the front of a draped table, or you can get a full table cover. For outdoor events, there are banners available in fabrics that resist rain and other elements. The cost of purchasing a banner or table drape generally depends upon its size, fabric, and type (such as designed banner with graphics, straight text, or stitched). You can purchase a banner for only a few hundred dollars. Appendix G identifies some suppliers of banners and displays.

At most events a six-foot or eight-foot table is usually provided. So make sure you don't forget to bring either your banner or display to career events so that you can easily be identified. A list of other "must bring" items appears in Figure 8–1.

Figure 8–1 Job Event Tips

BE SURE TO BRING THE FOLLOWING ITEMS:
- ☐ display, banner, or table drape
- ☐ job announcements/descriptions
- ☐ job application forms
- ☐ information about the library and its parent organization
- ☐ business cards
- ☐ pens
- ☐ stapler or paper clips
- ☐ file folders (to keep applications for different positions separated)
- ☐ calendar (if scheduling interview appointments during the event)

TIPS FOR BOOTH STAFF
1. Prior to the event, familiarize yourself with:
   - the positions for which you are recruiting
   - the salary and benefits of the positions
   - the specific working environment of the position
   - the application and selection process
   - specific deadline dates and other timelines
   - positive aspects of the library as an employer
2. Standard business attire should be worn. You want to appear as the professional you are.
3. Wear comfortable shoes—you may be standing for hours on end.
4. Be sure to wear your name badge so that applicants can easily address you.
5. Remember your etiquette—no eating, smoking, or the like at the booth. Don't carry on conversations with other booth staff when an individual approaches your booth.
6. Acknowledge each individual that stops by your booth—especially during busy periods.
7. Remember to smile as you great each person who stops by your booth. You want to reinforce the library's image as a friendly, welcoming place to work.
8. Speak clearly. It can be very noisy at the event.
9. Don't rely on your memory. Write down any specific information about applicants, their requests, or questions you need to act upon or respond to after the event. Failure to respond to an applicant's request reflects poorly upon the organization.

FIVE FATAL CAREER EVENT MISTAKES
1. Running out of applications or job announcements.
2. Not having your best staff/representatives work the career events.
3. Not treating all applicants the same.
4. Not having an easy way for applicants to identify who you are.
5. Not having enough staff for continuous event coverage.

3. PURCHASE EVENT-RELATED ADVERTISING SPACE

Many commercially produced job fairs issue an official career- or event-specific publication. The publication is distributed either to potential participants in advance of the event and/or to job seekers on site at the event. It invariably includes a list of all the employers participating in the event, but you can also buy space for display ads for a fee that ranges from $1,000 to $2,000 for a full-page, color ad. The job fair producer may also arrange for a special display-ad section in the local newspaper at a discounted fee. Job seekers are more likely to take greater notice and interest in employers who run display ads to those whose name only appears in a list of employers. However, if you do not have camera-ready, color or black-and-white display ads already developed, you need to seriously consider if your expected return (the acquisition of applications from significant numbers of quality applicants) is worth the investment of developing and placing the ad.

4. SEND A DIRECT MAILING TO PARTICIPANTS

If you plan to recruit at a professional conference or trade show, consider a direct mailing to preregistrants of the event to call attention to your presence at the event and to enable you to reach a larger audience than just those individuals who stop by your booth or table. Since the mailings of other employers and vendors will be vying for the registrants' attention, be sure the literature you intend to mail is well developed and competitive. Remember you are trying to leave a good impression and motivate your recipients to action.

5. BRING SUFFICIENT AND WELL-TRAINED BOOTH STAFF

Make sure you have sufficient staff available to staff your booth—at minimum two people, preferably four, and more than four the best option. Participation in these events is exhausting. You are constantly talking, answering questions, promoting the library or job openings, and trying to attract job seekers to your booth. You never want to leave your booth unstaffed, so you need at least two people to cover each other for lunch or a break. Because of the intensity of the work, however, most corporate employers utilize a four- to six-member crew. Half the crew works during morning hours, and a fresh crew comes in to work the afternoon.

Most libraries do not have a large enough personnel or human resources department staff to be able to spare four to six people to work a job event. So you need to put together a team that pairs a member of your personnel office with a member of your public services or public relations staff. Make sure that all staff working at the event are trained and knowledgeable about the library, its organization, career opportunitics, specific job vacancies, and the qualifications for those openings. The staff should also be good communicators, service oriented, good library ambassadors, and good salespeople.

6. OFFER SPECIAL ACTIVITIES AND GIVEAWAYS

If you have had the opportunity recently to stroll through a college or commercially produced job fair, you will have noticed that some employers were distributing premiums or giveaways. These giveaways attract participants to your booth—everyone likes getting something for free. However, my experience has been that premiums often draw a lot of "grabbers" to your booth. These are individuals who quickly walk by and grab a premium while trying to avoid talking to the booth staff. Unfortunately, they're very successful at it.

I've found that the use of giveaways in conjunction with an activity is more effective. For example, what has worked for us in the past is having participants answer a question about the library or library profession correctly in order to receive a giveaway. One of the problems we faced when we participated in a high-tech industry job fair was that the job seeker walking by our booth assumed that, since we were a library, we were only looking for librarians, even though we had job notices on the table for computer and technical positions. Utilizing a quiz and giveaways, we were able to attract job seekers to our booth, inform them about appropriate job openings at the library, and educate them about career opportunities in libraries. Our quiz consisted of one to three questions, depending upon how busy our booth traffic was, that asked about our library, library careers, or libraries in general. We drew some of the questions from the "quotable facts" brochure used in the ALA Advocacy Now! campaign. So many job seekers were amazed that there were more libraries than McDonald's nationwide! In terms of numbers, libraries cannot be ignored as employers.

Seven Tips On Purchasing Premiums and Giveaways

1. If you plan to purchase giveaway items, the items should in some way promote the library or library employment. For example, when we used paper airplanes as giveaways, we had them imprinted with the message, "Soar to New Heights with a Library Career." Be sure any imprinted giveaways include your library name on them.

2. Try to purchase giveaway items that match or complement the colors used in your display. Prior to placing an order, request a sample of the product in the color you desire. This insures you will have a proper color match and no unwarranted surprises.

3. Be alert to items that may be shipped unassembled (such as water bottles). If you select an item that requires assembly, check with the vendor to see if they will ship the items assembled for a

fee. Or else be sure to have adequate staff resources to assemble the products.

4. If you decide to order pencils as giveaways, but you also intend to use them in your booth for applicants to fill out forms, be sure you order sharpened pencils. The fee for these are slightly higher than for unsharpened pencils.

5. Make sure you have sufficient storage space for the giveaways. You get the best prices by ordering large quantities. Although 5,000 balloons may fit into one file cabinet drawer, 5,000 frisbees will require a larger storage area.

6. If you order large or fragile items such as mugs or candy jars, be aware of the extra care and effort needed to transport those items to career events.

7. If ordering edible items, make sure the items will be used within a few weeks of delivery. Cookies and chocolates do not stay fresh for any length of time. (Nothing leaves a bad impression like biting into a stale cookie.)

Appendix H provides a selected list of suppliers for giveaways and premiums.

AVOID THE FIVE FATAL JOB-EVENT MISTAKES

A lot of your time will be devoted to preplanning and preparing for job events. An ever greater amount of staff time and budget resources will need to be devoted to the actual events. So you need to do everything possible to ensure a successful outing. You need to make sure these events work for the library, not against it. To mitigate potential image disasters at these events, you need to avoid the five following basic fatal event mistakes.

1. *Failing to bring sufficient copies of job announcements/description and applications to the event.* Since these are job events, job seekers expect to be able to secure information about job openings. If your supply of announcements and applications is exhausted during the event, why are you there? You want to make it easy for potential applicants to apply for vacant positions. This includes giving them the necessary materials to do so. Although most job seekers at these events will arrive armed with ample copies of their resume for your review, if your li-

brary or parent organization requires submission of an official application, make sure you have more than enough copies for distribution. Since recruitment is a competitive activity, the well-prepared employer is the one who will ultimately recruit the best applicants.

2. *Failing to provide any signage to identify who you are.* Applicants need to be able to easily identify the employers. No one feels comfortable seeking employment with a no-name, unidentifiable employer.

3. *Failing to have continuous staffing at your booth/table.* You can't expect to catch fish without going fishing.

4. *Failing to have your best staff/representatives working the job event.* The potential applicants who approach your booth will be evaluating your library based in part on the staff at the booth. In the backs of their minds they'll be considering whether your booth staff are the type of people they'd like to work with. If they're alienated by your staff, don't expect them to come rushing to your door with their application.

5. *Failing to treat all potential applicants the same.* Remember that you're promoting not only your vacancies and the library as an employer, but also the library as a whole. Everyone deserves the same basic level of respect and service. At one career event I attended, the staff at a big computer industry employer's booth selectively handed out T-shirts to applicants. Needless to say, this unequal treatment was quickly noticed and commented upon by job seekers.

Although participation in job events is intensive and exhausting, it's also fun. Don't be afraid to try new and creative ways to draw desirable applicants to your booth. And always make the time to walk the event floor to see what other employers are doing that draw applicants to their booths.

To get an idea of costs connected with exhibiting at an activity, see page 89.

Worksheet: Associated Activity Costs

Not all of the costs listed may apply to your specific circumstances.

PURCHASING EVENT-RELATED ADVERTISING SPACE

Development of a display advertisement

Graphic artist/design fees = $_____

Photography fees = $_____

Production fees (black and white) = $_____

Production fees (color) = $_____

Camera-ready copy fee = $_____

                                        Subtotal = $_____

Advertisement publication fees

Event guide = $_____

Newspaper = $_____

Radio = $_____

Subtotal = $_____

                              Total Advertising = $_____

Direct Mail

Purchase of mailing labels of preregistrants = $_____

Mailing reproduction fees = $_____

Postage = $_____

                              Total Direct Mail = $_____

SPECIAL ACTIVITIES AND GIVEAWAYS

Printing or reproduction costs = $_____

Special supply costs = $_____

Giveaway products

Product purchase cost = $_____

Imprinting cost = $_____

Assembly cost = $_____

Shipping cost = $_____

                                        Subtotal = $_____

                       Total Promotions/Giveaways = $_____

9 NETWORKING FOR RECRUITMENT PURPOSES

In many ways, recruiting good library staff is as difficult as recruiting new pro football players. Both arenas have talented players heavily engaged in their work who usually don't have the time to shop around for a new team to play on. So you, like pro coaches, have to identify, seek out, and recruit these talented individuals. If you think you can walk up to pro players in any profession, introduce yourself, tell them about an opening, and expect them immediately to sign on, you must be dreaming. You have to find an opportunity, and then a means to interact with these players to determine if they truly possess the characteristics you seek. The key to gaining access to, and interacting with these potential players, or applicants, is networking.

UNDERSTAND THE PURPOSE OF NETWORKING

Networking serves several recruitment purposes. It provides you with a professional social environment where you can become acquainted with a large group of people. It presents you with an opportunity personally to identify potential, competitive applicants for current or future vacancies. Through your interaction with these individuals, you have several occasions to assess informally their suitability or competitiveness for specific vacancies. And after identifying suitable applicants, networking also gives you a way to try to motivate the individuals into submitting an application for employment. You have an opportunity to talk one-on-one with potential applicants prior to and outside of the formal interview process, which generally gives you a sense of the character and potential "fit" of applicants that you can't get from advertisement sources.

FOLLOW THE FIVE BASIC STEPS IN RECRUITMENT NETWORKING

Recruitment networking is not a haphazard activity. Like other recruitment activities, if conducted properly, it can be a very productive means of yielding quality applicants. But if poorly done, it can have a negative impact on your efforts. Productive networking includes several basic activities or steps.

STEP 1. IDENTIFY LIKE-MINDED ORGANIZATIONS

Search out organizations, associations, or groups whose membership is likely to consist of desired applicants, and look for a local or regional chapter in your area. Go back and review your list of current and future vacancies to see the types of positions you are trying to fill. If you're seeking computer people, you'll be seeking out organizations or associations comprised of technical or computer people, or groups of individuals who share an interest in computing. As you identify appropriate associations, don't overlook your local service clubs like the Rotary or Lions Clubs. These organizations have a varied membership that includes professionals in various fields with a dedication to community service.

STEP 2. JOIN THE ORGANIZATION

In joining, you gain a better sense of the organization, its members, and its publications. You'll be able to interact with members of the group at meetings, conferences, and other events. You'll also have the opportunity to learn who these members are employed by, and who these competitors are. Expect to attend meetings over a continued course of time. Networking for recruitment is an ongoing process.

STEP 3. ESTABLISH CREDIBILITY

It is vital to establish your credibility as an individual and as a recruiter. Remember those movies where a con artist pulls out a business card, hands it to a stranger, then immediately tries to sell that person something? Well, this is exactly what you want to avoid doing. Be aware of any informal meeting etiquette rules—don't seize upon the first meeting to try and recruit applicants. Take some time to establish your personal credibility through your employment, education, experience, and accomplishments. Taking this time will also allow you to acquaint yourself with members who may be potential applicants. And don't forget that you are an ambassador from the library, so look for opportunities where you or the library can be of benefit to the organization.

STEP 4. KNOW YOUR LIBRARY

Be well versed in and informed about all aspects of the library. Although you are well versed in all aspects of the library as an employer, be prepared when one or more members ask you a question about the library, its services, collections, program, hours, and so forth. Providing answers to their questions will help you establish your credibility, whereas providing inaccurate or misinformation can damage both the library's and your image and credibility.

STEP 5. PROMOTE THE LIBRARY OVERALL

Look for opportunities to promote the library not only as an employer, but also as a resource. You'll recognize these appropriate opportunities. Just be alert to them when they present themselves.

TOOLS OF THE RECRUITING TRADE

As you begin, or continue your recruitment networking efforts, always be sure you have the following two tools at hand: business cards, and a library contact list. The list should include the telephone and fax numbers and e-mail addresses of the various library units or staff members to contact for answers to a variety of questions ranging from renewing a book over the phone to the library's Internet filtering policy.

As you begin your efforts to network for recruitment purposes, you may also want to consider finding opportunities to network with other recruiters in the area. There are generally local or regional organizations of employers or recruiters. Participation in these organizations or attendance at their meetings can provide you with valuable recruitment ideas and tips.

APPENDIX A: EXECUTIVE SEARCH FIRMS, CONSULTING AND PLACEMENT SERVICES

These firms and services handle library and/or public sector positions.

Advanced Information Management
444 Castro St., Suite 320
Mountain View, CA 94041
(650) 965-7799

Ralph Andersen & Associates
4240 Rocklin Rd., Suite 11
Rocklin, CA 95677
(916) 630-4900

C. Berger & Co.
P.O. Box 274
Wheaton, IL 60189
(800) 382-4222 or (630) 653-1115
www.cberger.com

David M. Griffith & Associates
630 Dundee Rd., Suite 200
Northbrook, IL 60062
(847) 564-9270

Library Co-Op Inc.
3840 Park Ave., Suite 107
Edison, NJ 08820
(800) 654-6275

Oldani Group, Inc.
188 106th Ave., NE, Suite 420
Bellevue, WA 98004
(425) 451-3938
www.theoldanigroup.com

Pro Libra Associates Inc.
6 Inwood Place
Maplewood, NJ 07040
(800) 262-0070 or (903) 762-0070

APPENDIX B: SELECTED LIST OF PERIODICALS THAT CARRY LIBRARY JOB ADVERTISEMENTS

Affirmative Action Register
Contact:
Affirmative Action Register
8356 Olive Blvd.
St. Louis, MO 63132
(800) 537-0655 or (314) 991-1335
Monthly publication. Accepts both classified and display ads. Ad rates can be requested from publisher online at www/aar-eeo.com or by e-mail to aareeo@concentric.net.
Circulation: over 62,500.

American Libraries
Contact:
Career Leeds
American Libraries
50 E. Huron St.
Chicago, IL 60611
(800) 545-2433 or (312) 280-4216
Monthly publication. Accepts both classified and display ads.
Circulation: over 59,000.

The Chronicle of Higher Education
Contact:
Bulletin Board
The Chronicle of Higher Education
1255 23rd St., N.W.
Washington, D.C. 20037
(202) 466-1050
Weekly publication. Accepts both classified and display ads. Rate information, issue dates, and deadlines are accessible on the Web at chronicle.merit.edu/about-help.dir/bb-ad.html
Circulation: over 93,000.

College and Research Libraries
Contact:
Classified Ads Manager
College and Research Libraries
50 E. Huron St.
Chicago, IL 60611
(800) 545-2433, ext. 2513
Monthly publication. Accepts both classified and display ads. Rate information and issue dates and deadlines accessible on the Web at www.ala.org/acrl/adver2.html
Circulation: over 11,900.

Information Outlook
Contact:
Special Libraries Association
1700 Eighteenth St., NW
Washington, D.C. 20009-2514
(301) 963-3622
Monthly publication. Accepts both classified and display ads. Rate card, issue dates, and deadlines are accessible on the Web at www.sla.org/pubs/serial/rate.html
Circulation: over 15,000.

Library Hotline
Contact: Library Hotline
245 West 17th St.
New York, NY 10011
(212) 463-6774
Weekly publication. Accepts both classified and display ads.

Library Journal
Contact:
Special Marketing and Sales Dept.
Library Journal
245 W. 17th St.
New York, NY 10011
(800) 523-9654, (212) 463-6819
Semimonthly publication. Accepts both classified and display ads.
Circulation: over 22,500.

Library Mosaics
Contact:
Library Mosaics
P.O. Box 5171
Culver City, CA 90231
(310) 410-1573
Bimonthly publication. Accepts classified ads. Contact the magazine for advertising rates. Circulation: over 5,000. (Target audience of this publication is library support staff.)

LITA (Library and Information Technology Association) Newsletter
Published in electronic format only.
Contact:
Library and Information Technology Association
(a division of the American Library Association)
50 E. Huron St.
Chicago, IL 60611
(800) 545-2433, ext. 4270
Newsletter is published quarterly, however job ads are posted weekly. Rate and submission information is accessible on the Web at www.lita.org/jobs/jobs.cgi

APPENDIX C: ASSOCIATIONS OPERATING JOB LINES

NATIONAL ASSOCIATIONS

American Association of Law Libraries
53 W. Jackson Blvd., Suite 940
Chicago, IL 60604
(312) 939-4764

Medical Library Association
6 N. Michigan Ave., Suite 300
Chicago, IL 60602
(312) 419-9094

Special Libraries Association
1700 Eighteenth St., N.W.
Washington, DC 20009
(202) 234-4700

Several regional chapters of the Special Libraries Association also operate job lines.

STATE ASSOCIATIONS

California Library Association
717 "K" St., Suite 300
Sacramento, CA
(916) 447-8541

Connecticut Library Association
Franklin Commons
106 Route 32
Franklin, CT 06254
(860) 889-1200

Illinois Library Association
33 W. Grand, Suite 301
Chicago, IL 60610
(312) 644-1896

Maryland Library Association
400 Cathedral St., 3rd Fl.
Baltimore, MD 21201
(410) 727-7422

Michigan Library Association
6810 S. Cedar, #6
Lansing, MI 48911
(517) 694-6615

Missouri Library Association
1306 Business 63 S., Suite B
Columbia, MO 65201-8404
(573) 449-4627

New Jersey Library Association
P. O. Box 1534
Trenton, NJ 08607
(609) 394-8032

New York Library Association
252 Hudson Ave.
Albany, NY 12210-1802
(518) 432-6952

Texas Library Association
3355 Bee Cave Rd., Suite 401
Austin, TX 78746
(512) 328-1518

Virginia Library Association
P. O. Box 8277
Norfolk, VA 23503
(757) 583-0041

APPENDIX D: SELECTED LISTSERVS

Note: Check with the list administrator as to whether, and under what conditions, job announcements may be posted on their listservs. In general, only subscribers of a listserv are allowed to post messages to the list.

LISTSERVS TARGETED AT PROVIDING INFORMATION ON LIBRARY JOBS

ACRLNY-L@LISTS.NYUEDU
    To subscribe, send:
        subscribe ACRLNY-L your name
        to LISTPROC@LISTS.NYU.EDU
LIBJOBS@INFOSERV.NLC-BNC.CA
    To subscribe, send:
        subscribe LIBJOBS your name
        to LISTSERV@INFOSERV.NLC-BNC.CA

SPECIAL INTEREST LISTSERVS

CHILDREN'S LIBRARIANSHIP
PUBYAC@NYSERNET.ORG
    To subscribe, send:
        subscribe PUBYAC your name
        to MAJORDOMO@NYSERNET.ORG

LAW LIBRARIANSHIP
LAW-LIB@UCDAVIS.EDU
    To subscribe, send:
        subscribe LAWLIB your name
        to LISTPROC@UCDAVIS.EDU

LIBRARY ADMINISTRATION AND MANAGEMENT

LIBADMIN@LIST.AB.UMD.EDU
> To subscribe, send:
>> subscribe LIBAMIN your name
>> to LISTPROC@LIST.AB.UMD.EDU

MEDICAL LIBRARIANSHIP

MEDLIB-L@UBVM.CC.BUFFALO.EDU
> To subscribe, send:
>> subscribe MEDLIB-L your name
>> to LISTSERV@UBVM.CC.BUFFALO.EDU

PUBLIC LIBRARIANSHIP

PUBLIB@SUNSITE.BERKELEY.EDU
> To subscribe, send:
>> subscribe PUBLIB@SUNSITE.BERKELEY.EDU
>> to LISTSERV@SUNSITE.BERKELEY.EDU

REFERENCE LIBRARIANSHIP

LIBREF-L@LISTSERV.KENT.EDU
> To subscribe, send:
>> subscribe LIBREF-L your name
>> to LISTSERV@LISTSERV.KENT.EDU

MARS-L@ALA.ORG
> To subscribe, send:
>> subscribe MARS-L your name
>> to LISTPROC@ALA.ORG

SPECIAL COLLECTIONS, ARCHIVAL, AND RARE BOOK LIBRARIANSHIP

ARCHIVES@MIAMU.MUOHIO.EDU
> To subscribe, send:
>> subscribe ARCHIVES your name
>> to LISTSERV@MIAMIU.MUOHIO.EDU

CONSDIST@LINDY.STANFORD.EDU
> To subscribe, send:
>> subscribe CONSDIST your name
>> to SONSDIST-REQUEST@LINDY.STANFORD.EDU

EXLIBRIS@LIBRARY.BERKELEY.EDU
> To subscribe, send:
>> subscribe EXLIBRIS your name
>> to LISTPROC@LIBRARY.BERKELEY.EDU

LIS-RAREBOOKS@MAILBASE.AC.UK
>   To subscribe, send:
>>   subscribe LIS-RAREBOOKS your name
>>   to MAILBASE@MAILBASE.AC.UK

VRA-L@UAFSYSB.UARK.EDU
>   To subscribe, send:
>>   subscribe VRA-L your name
>>   to LISTSERV@UAFSYSB.UARK.EDU

FOR SUPPORT STAFF

LIBSUP-L@U.WASHINGTON.EDU
>   To subscribe, send:
>>   subscribe LIBSUP-L your name
>>   to LISTPROC@U.WASHINGTON.EDU

TECHNOLOGY: DIGITAL, INTERNET, AND OTHER

ASIS-L@ASIS.ORG
>   To subscribe, send:
>>   subscribe ASIS-L your name
>>   to LISTSERV@ASIS.ORG

DIGLIBNS@SUNSITE.BERKELEY.EDU
>   To subscribe, send:
>>   subscribe DIGLIBNS your name
>>   to LISTSERV@SUNSITE.BERKELEY.EDU

PUBLIB-NET@SUNSITE.BERKELEY.EDU
>   To subscribe, send:
>>   subscribe PUBLIB-NET your name
>>   to LISTSERV@SUNSITE.BERKELEY.EDU

SYSLIB-L@LISTSERV.ACSU.BUFFALO.EDU
>   To subscribe, send:
>>   subscribe SYSLIB-L your name
>>   to LISTSERV@ACSU.BUFFALO.EDU

WEB4LIB@SUNSITE.BERKELEY.EDU
>   To subscribe, send:
>>   subscribe WEB4LIB your name
>>   to LISTSERV@SUNSITE.BERKELEY.EDU

APPENDIX E: WEB SITES OF ASSOCIATIONS LISTING JOB OPPORTUNITIES

American Association of Law Libraries
  www.aallnet.org

American Library Association
  www.ala.org

Black Caucus of the American Library Association
  www.bcala.org

Library and Information Technology Association
  www.lita.org

Special Libraries Association
  www.sla.org

Medical Library Association
  www.mlanet.org

APPENDIX F:
SELECTED JOB SITES
ON THE WEB

The following are examples of some of the many Web sites containing employment listings.

America's Job Bank
www.ajb.dni.us

CareerMosaic
www.careermosaic.com

CareerPath
www.careerpath.com

JOBTRAK
www.jobtrak.com

The Monster Board
www.monster.com

The Online Career Center
www.occ.com

Yahoo Classifieds
classifieds.yahoo.com

APPENDIX G: SELECTED LIST OF DISPLAY AND BANNER SUPPLIERS

DISPLAYS

Abex Display Systems
7101 Fair Ave.
North Hollywood, CA 91605
(800) 537-0231
www.abex.com

Channel-Kor Systems
P.O. Box 2297
Bloomington, IN 47402
(812) 336-7599

Featherlight Exhibits
7300 32nd Ave., N.
Minneapolis, MN 55427-2885
(800) 229-5533
www.featherlight.com

Godfrey Group, Inc.
P.O. Box 90008
Raleigh, NC 27675-0008
(919) 544-6504

Impact Displays
2570 Lafayette St.
Santa Clara, CA 95050
(888) 988-2131

Nimlok Company
7420 N. Lehigh Ave.
Niles, IL 60714-9878
(800) 233-8870
www.nimlock.com

Nomadic Display
7400 Fullerton Rd.
Springfield, VA 22153-2831
(800) 732-9395
www.nomadicdisplay.com

Professional Exhibits and Graphics
1188 Bordeaux Dr.
Sunnyvale, CA 94089
(800) 734-0064
www.proexhibits.com

Skyline Displays Bay Area
305 Soquel Way
Sunnyvale, CA 94086
(408) 524-2440
www.skylinedisplays.com

TigerMark Exhibit Systems
21 Blandin Ave.
Framingham, MA 01701
(800) 338-8465
www.tigermark.com

BANNERS AND TABLE DRAPES

Banner Impressions
125 North Beacon St.
Boston, MA 02135-9870
(800) 922-1892
www.bannerimp.com

Carrot-Top Industries Inc.
328 Elizabeth Brady Rd.
P.O. Box 820
Hillsborough, NC 27278
(800) 628-3524

Kalamazoo Banner Works
2129 Portage St.
Kalamazoo, MI 49001-6198
(888) 254-7744

New England Flag & Banner
125 North Beacon St.
Boston, MA 02135
(800) 922-1892

APPENDIX H: SELECTED LIST OF SUPPLIERS OF PREMIUMS AND GIVEAWAYS

The Adcap Line
1400 Goldmine Rd.
Monroe, NC 28110
(800) 868-7111
www.adcap.com

Best Impressions
P.O. Box 802
LaSalle, IL 61301
(800) 635-2378
www.bestimpressions. com

Competitive Edge
3500 109th St.
Des Moines, IA 50322
(800) 458-3343

Crestline Company, Inc.
P.O. Box 2027
Mt. Hope Ave.
Lewiston, ME 04241
(800) 221-7797

JanWay Company
11 Academy Rd.
Cogan Station, PA 17728-9300
(800) 877-5342
www.janway.com

Promotional Products Unlimited
2291 W. 205th St., Suite 201
Torrance, CA 90501
(800) 748-6150

Sales Guides, International
P.O. Box 64784
St. Paul, MN 55164–0784
(800) 352-9899

Success Builders
600 Academy Dr.
Northbrook, IL 60062–2430
(800) 231–2332
www. BaldwinCooke.com

BIBLIOGRAPHY

Berenson, Conrad, and Henry O. Rhunke. *Job Descriptions: How to Write and Use Them.* Swarthmore, PA: Personnel Journal, 1967.

Cook, Mary F., ed. *The AMA Handbook for Employee Recruitment and Retention.* San Francisco: American Management Association, 1992.

Curzon, Susan. *Managing the Interview.* New York: Neal-Schuman, 1995.

Dobrish, Cecelia, Rick Wolff, and Brian Zevnik. *Hiring the Right Person for the Right Job.* New York: Franklin Watts, 1984.

Fitz-Enz, Jac. "Highly Effective HR Practices: Copycatting Someone Else's Best Processes is Not Always the Best Practice." *HR FOCUS* (April) 1997: 11–12.

Fyock, Catherine D. "Expanding the Talent Search: 19 Ways to Recruit Top Talent." *HR Magazine* 36 (July 1991): 33–35.

Gaynor, Diane. "What Do You Want in Your Ads? Good Recruitment Ads Require Careful Preparation." *Real Estate Today* 23 (January/February 1990): 62–63.

Gootar, Selvin. "We Want You!" *Office Systems* (February 1998): 46–47.

Half, Robert. *Finding, Hiring, and Keeping the Best Employees.* New York: Wiley, 1993.

Holdeman, John B., Jeffrey, M. Aldridge, and David Jackson. "How to Hire Ms./Mr. Right." *Journal of Accountancy* 182 (August 1996): 55–57.

Litvan, Laura M. "Casting a Wider Employment Net." *Nation's Business* 82 (December 1994): 49–51.

Marlow, Paula. "Show Search: Selecting the Right Shows Is Science, Not Intuition: Locate the Best Choices with This Five Step Process." *Exhibitor* 16 (October 1997): 32–36.

Matthews, Marianne. "If Your Ads Aren't Pulling Top Sales Talent...The Problem Could Be You've Forgotten the Sales Pitch." *Sales & Marketing Management* 142 (February 1990): 75–80.

Mornell, Pierre. *45 Effective Ways for Hiring Smart! How to Predict Winners and Losers in the Incredibly Expensive People-Reading Game.* Berkeley, CA: Ten Speed Press, 1998.

Pell, Arthur R. *Recruiting and Selecting Personnel.* New York: Regents Publishing, 1969.

Rubin, Richard D. *Hiring Library Employees.* New York: Neal-Schuman, 1993.

Spragins, Ellyn E. "Hiring Without the Guesswork." *Inc.* 14 (Feburary 1992): 80–89.

Terpstra, David E. "Recruitment and Selection: The Search for Effective Methods." *HR FOCUS* (May 1996): 16–17.

Walters, Suzanne. *Customer Service*. New York: Neal-Schuman, 1994.

Wendover, Robert W. *High Performance Hiring*. Los Altos, CA: Crisp Publications, 1991.

Wheatley, Malcolm. "The Talent Spotters." *Management Today* (June 1996): 62.

Whiteman-Jones, Michael. "Hiring and Keeping the Best: The 10 Commandments." *Colorado Business Magazine* 20 (October 1993): 45.

Wolfe, Lisa A. *Library Public Relations, Promotions, and Communications*. New York: Neal-Schuman, 1997.

Yate, Martin John. *Hiring the Best: A Manager's Guide to Effective Interviewing*. Holbrook, MA: Bob Adams, 1988.

INDEX

ABOUT THE AUTHOR

Kathleen Low has held numerous positions in the California State Library. Presently she is the human resources development consultant in the Library Development Services Bureau of the state library.

During her employment with the Library Development Services Bureau, she has developed and implemented a number of statewide targeted grant programs focusing on various human resources issues such as staff development and recruitment. She also initiated a recruitment campaign that won a John Cotton Dana Award for public relations.

Low has written numerous articles and a previous book. She holds a B.A. in Spanish from the University of California at Davis and an MLS from San Jose (Calif.) State University.